Woman

With love & prayers,
Diane Allanson

Woman

Diane Sillaman

authorHOUSE®

AuthorHouse™
1663 Liberty Drive
Bloomington, IN 47403
www.authorhouse.com
Phone: 1-800-839-8640

© *2012 by Diane Sillaman. All rights reserved.*

No part of this book may be reproduced, stored in a retrieval system, or transmitted by any means without the written permission of the author.

First published by AuthorHouse   01/25/2012

ISBN: 978-1-4685-4650-7 (sc)
ISBN: 978-1-4685-4649-1 (hc)
ISBN: 978-1-4685-4648-4 (ebk)

Library of Congress Control Number: 2012901300

Printed in the United States of America

Any people depicted in stock imagery provided by Thinkstock are models, and such images are being used for illustrative purposes only.
Certain stock imagery © Thinkstock.

This book is printed on acid-free paper.

Because of the dynamic nature of the Internet, any web addresses or links contained in this book may have changed since publication and may no longer be valid. The views expressed in this work are solely those of the author and do not necessarily reflect the views of the publisher, and the publisher hereby disclaims any responsibility for them.

Contents

CHAPTER ONE
    THE BEGINNING 1
        Discussion Questions 4
CHAPTER TWO
    VERY GOOD TIMES 5
        Discussion Questions 7
CHAPTER THREE
    PARADISE LOST 9
        Discussion Questions 14
CHAPTER FOUR
    CONSEQUENCE AND PROMISE 16
        Discussion Questions 22
CHAPTER FIVE
    THE WOMAN LOOKS FOR HELP 23
        Discussion Questions 26
CHAPTER SIX
    GOD SEES AND KNOWS 27
        Discussion Questions 33
CHAPTER SEVEN
    GOD ANNOUNCES TO A WOMAN 34
        Discussion Questions 41
CHAPTER EIGHT
    NABAL AND ABIGAIL 42
        Discussion Questions 44

CHAPTER NINE
    NABAL AND ABIGAIL PART 2 46
        Discussion Questions 55
CHAPTER TEN
    THE PROMISED SEED..56
        Discussion Questions 59
CHAPTER ELEVEN
    THE SEED IN EARLY LIFE 60
        Discussion Questions 65
CHAPTER TWELVE
    JESUS, UNIQUE AMONG MEN 66
        Discussion Questions 69
CHAPTER THIRTEEN
    JESUS AND A CANAANITE WOMAN 70
        Discussion Questions 73
CHAPTER FOURTEEN
    A BLEEDING WOMAN'S TESTIMONY
    (FROM LUKE 8:43-38)...74
        Discussion Questions 77
CHAPTER FIFTEEN
    AN ADULTEROUS WOMAN(JOHN 8:1-11)...............78
        Discussion Questions 84
CHAPTER SIXTEEN
    A SOCIAL OUTCAST (JOHN 4).................................86
        Discussion Questions 92
CHAPTER SEVENTEEN
    THE WOMAN WITH THE OINTMENT
    (MATT. 26:6-13, MARK 14:3-9,
    LUKE 7:36-50, JOHN 12:1-8) 93
        Discussion Questions 99

Chapter Eighteen
   WOMEN AND JESUS 101
      Discussion Questions 106
Chapter Nineteen
   WOMAN'S ROLE IN WINNING THE WORLD..............107
      Discussion Questions 111
Chapter Twenty
   MY WALK WITH JESUS 112
      Author's Note 119

Chapter One

The Beginning

I want you to go on a journey through time with me back several thousand years to what the Bible says is the beginning. It is dark. The earth is a nebulous mass. We sense a spirit hovering over the waters. We hear a voice saying, "Let there be light!" A beautiful, pure, lovely, good light shines forth. The darkness is separated from the light. The light is named Day and the darkness is named Night. The first day ever in earth's history is complete.

The second day an expanse separates water from water, over from under. The expanse is called Sky. It is good. There is evening and there is morning and the second day ends.

The third day dry land is brought forth and plants appear all over it: beautiful, lovely, varied living green things from grasses to trees of all types, all with seeds that would reproduce each plant after its kind. All the earth formed that day was covered with lush, wonderful vegetation. Fruits, vegetables, flowers. It was all good.

Diane Sillaman

The fourth day the sun, moon, and stars in all their glory were made. The moon was to govern the night, the sun to govern the day. The stars were amazing, billions in glorious array stretching far into the expanse of space. The night sky was glorious. These heavenly bodies made possible the tracking of time: days, months, seasons, and years. Plants met the Sun the day after they were formed. They already had light. Isn't that creative? It is also quiet, just the sound of growing plants, maybe breezes blowing through the branches of balsam trees, maybe the sound of lapping waves on the shoreline. It was all good. Evening and morning marked this fourth day also.

The fifth day birds and fish are made. The waters teem with life from the microscopic to the huge blue whale, from the creeping octopus to the happy dolphins. The waters are active, amazing places now. Parrots, bluebirds, robins, eagles, and every other kind of bird fill the forests, jungles, and sky with their color, flight and songs. It is a good day.

When the next day begins, animals come forth into their first existence. There were elephants, moles, horses, pigs, alligators, monkeys, dinosaurs, snakes, dogs, giraffes, and rhinoceros. Movement, noises, more color. Everything ate plants. It was good. The earth was full of life and beauty. The skies and seas were also. What a wonderful planet! If the creation would have stopped there, the earth would have been the most glorious zoological gardens, perfect in its setting in the universe. But the Creator was not done. There had to be someone to appreciate it all, to love the beauty, to enjoy the sounds, to study the expansive array of created things, and to look after the welfare of the various creatures and plants on the earth. "Let us make man in our image, in our likeness, and let them rule over the fish of the sea and the birds of the air, over the livestock, over all the earth, and over all the creatures that move along the ground." So the Creator forms the first man out of the soil of the earth and breathes into his nostrils. The man comes to life, a special hand-made creation of God. For the first time since all began something is not good. It is not good for the man to be alone.

The Creator brought all the animals to the man to see what he would call each kind. What an intelligent creature! He had the gift of language right from the start, with quite a vocabulary!

By the way, people have been making up names for things ever since, naming both things found in creation and things that mankind has made. We cannot seem to help ourselves. Much of education is simply learning the names of things so that communication is clear.

After he had met and named all the creatures, it was clear that there was no one like him. Male and female of all the other creatures were together and thriving, but there was no one for him to be with.

The Creator caused a deep sleep to come on the man. While he was asleep, God took one of his ribs and formed a female human, beautiful and lovely. God brought her to the man. She was the crown of all creation, the last creature made. The man and the woman were made in the image of God. They had language, personality, great abilities to govern and understand. They could be creative with the created order making music and art, rearranging things into gardens. Their work was a delight. Everything they needed was already there. They lived in a wonderland of beauty and goodness. Only after the creation of man *and* woman was the creation complete and called "very good."

Discussion Questions

1. Describe what you think a day in the life of Eve may have been like before the fall.

2. Have you ever given thought to the power it would take to create a single star? God made billions. How does it make you feel about God that He used His tremendous power to make a world like this one?

Chapter Two

Very Good Times

It would be wise for us to just watch for a while and see this wonderful place in action. We will recognize it, I think . . . not because we have ever seen it, but because we dream of it. We humans have written and sung about, longed for and believed in a perfect existence. We cannot seem to help it. Even our negative speech about the world as it is now reveals that we know something has been lost. We firmly believe that life is not fair, that things should not be this way. Let's look with our imaginations at what the earliest history of Earth was like after this point of completion.

The Bible says that on the seventh day God rested from all His creative work. So the first full day of man and woman's existence, they were able to just be. They could revel in who they were, who He was, and all the perfection of the created things. There was so much to discover!

Can you imagine the total perfection of those days? The man and the woman understood each other perfectly. They both understood the Creator was magnificent and loving, personal and fun. I can just hear the laughter as they watched one of the first monkeys. I can feel their awe in watching a blue whale breach. The perfection of the birds' songs filled them with joy.

There was no fear, no hardship. Everything was provided free of charge. Nothing was ruined or lost. The relationships were all perfectly healthy between the two people, and between each of them and Creator God. To be perfectly loved, perfectly understood, perfectly able to be yourself without judgment or criticism is a longing which still beats in every human heart. The man and the woman both felt safe, like they belonged, were accepted and valued, and that they had a good purpose.

That very first day they simply rejoiced in who the Creator was and in who they were because He had made them. It was a restful, peaceful, beautiful day. That was the seventh day of earth's history. The first week was ended.

It is interesting to note that the earth's revolution around the sun marks the length of a year. The moon's revolution around the earth marks a month. The rotation of the earth on its axis marks a day, but no astronomical marking exists for a week. God gave us that pattern. He created for six days and rested on the seventh.

As the second week begins fresh and new, we see the man and the woman actively engaging the created order. Maybe they gathered various flowers to make an especially breath-taking garden. Perhaps they tasted a number of the vegetables, fruits and grains and tried to categorize them. They may have taught the dogs some tricks. Whatever they did, it was good work: fun, interesting, productive, and companionable.

They loved it! Getting up each day was a great adventure. They were afraid of nothing, careful about nothing. Everything they wanted to do was possible: no time pressure, no boss breathing down their necks, no shortage of things to do, no limit to their ability to do whatever they thought of doing, no frustration.

In their friendship with each other there was perfect respect and honor, perfect love and peace. There was no anger, no hurt feelings, no wounding, no confusion, no isolation, no pain, and no heartache. Think of the very best moments of your relationship with anyone; multiply that by thousands and take away any other type of moment and you might have a pale shadow of what their life with each other was like.

It was a beautiful world with beautiful people and things in it. The weather was perfect. There were no dangers, no worries, and no fears . . . a lovely, safe, rich world with sweet, happy people to oversee it. Above it all the most delightful, loving, creative, wonderful, perfect God who rejoiced in its creatures and enjoyed the company of the humans every evening as they walked in the gardens together, probably talking over the adventures of the day before settling down for peaceful, deep sleep. It was truly Paradise.

Discussion Questions

1. What are some "non-negotiables" in our view of Paradise? What would have to be there? What would have to not be there?

2. What does it say about God that the humans had absolutely everything they needed to thrive?

3. As Adam and Eve related to each other, what were some notable differences from the relationships of today? What do we long for?

Chapter Three

Paradise Lost

No study of woman would be complete without the information we have reviewed so far. She was made in the image of God, reflecting His innately relational character and His beauty. She enjoyed flawless relationships with everyone and everything. She was not at all worried, stressed, concerned about anything. She lived an interesting, happy, love-filled, secure, safe, fascinating life. She was intelligent, beautiful, athletic, healthy, unafraid, and unashamed. Her life was perfect. Indeed, it was as God said, "very good."

There is a resident longing for this actual historical experience in the heart of every woman born on the planet since that perfect beginning. If a woman is to be understood, it must be on the basis of what she was created to be, free in her valued role in the world at its inception. She was loved and cared for, loving, restful and caring. She was strong and gracious, delightful and lovely. Every woman bears the longing for these things to be true of her.

The story of the loss of all this is a sad one, but it ends with a promise. The beautiful world in its perfect setting in the solar system, galaxy and universe had one rule in it. Our world today has so many rules I doubt that an actual count could be made. But at the beginning in the state of "very good" there was only one, "Do not eat from the tree of the knowledge of good and evil."

Can you imagine a world where evil was not known? Most of the thoughtful women I know have a hard time accepting that God Himself is truly good because of the evil in the world. It is so pervasive in ours: evil between family members, neighbors, co-workers, tribes, nations, between man and nature. Everything that makes life so very difficult can be traced to evil in the world. Evil is not a good thing to know. And the purveyor of evil was crafty, hate-filled, and subtle. He was an enemy of the Creator of all this beautiful goodness. He became the first enemy of the ones uniquely created in the image of God, those God put in charge of caring for all the created things. He simply had to get them to eat of that fruit. Then they and their children to the end of time would know well what evil was.

So he appeared to Eve as a serpent in the branches of *that* tree and spoke to her. "Did God really say 'You must not eat from any tree in the garden?'" Can you believe it?!? How dare he cast such an accusation on the generous, loving, delightful, creative Artist who made an exquisitely lovely world . . . everything seen to, each plant, animal, fish and bird reproducing after its kind, all living things eating plants, perfect weather, and perfect harmony among them all. His "image bearers" could eat of any plant at all except for the one in which the serpent now reposed.

Eve answered him, "We may eat fruit from the trees of the garden, but God did say, 'You must not eat fruit from the tree in the middle of the garden, and you must not touch it, or you will die.'" The rule did not originally include touching the tree or its fruit. Can you see how the addition of that prohibition shows that Eve was toying with the idea that maybe she was being left out of something good? Maybe she was being treated unfairly. Such a subtle shift, but so significant. The One she had known and loved with Adam was now being looked at like an enemy, like an unjust rule maker. If she could have seen the horrible consequences all of her children down through the ages would live with because of the knowledge of evil, she probably would have tried to construct an impenetrable wall around the tree so that no one ever could have eaten of it. But she did not see.

"You will not surely die," says the serpent. In other words, "God has lied to you." The One who is true is being slurred. Such a twist! The one who lies perpetually is calling the One who is Truth a liar. Alarms should be going off in Eve's head right now! But she didn't know evil yet. She didn't know lies existed. She did know the One who is true, but now He is being covered from her view with a veil of deceit.

"For God knows that when you eat of it your eyes will be opened, you will be like God, knowing good and evil." You see how God's "angle" has been revealed. According to Satan, God just wants all this lovely knowledge to Himself. Knowledge is power, don't you know. Oh, that Eve would have seen through these lies and resisted! God is not evil. He is not selfish. His command to not eat from that tree was meant to protect the people, not rob them of some great thing!

Do you, my dear reader, think that the knowledge of evil is a good thing? Has it made life on this planet better to know that stealing, lying, cheating, murdering, dishonoring, coveting, etc. are possible? Can anyone speak up for the benefits of evil? Is there anything defensible in it?

The serpent is done. He has questioned God's motives, baited the hook with desire to be like God, and revealed that God is a liar and not to be trusted. He is now finished. There is not another word from him in this story. He has done what he came to do. The destruction is on the way.

Advertising, selling, and promoting use similar tactics. The wise know that there are such things as ulterior motives. The one thing that undoes any sales pitch is, "I am content with what I have." There is no argument to that. Eve could in all truth have said that. She had a perfect gentleman for a husband, a perfect job, a perfect home, a loving God, security, beauty, safety, and purpose. She had all that her daughters have been looking for ever since, but she didn't resist the pitch. She allowed discontent to make her vulnerable. She looked at the fruit, saw that it was good for food and pleasing to the eye and was also desirable for gaining wisdom. These three qualities have been tripping people up ever since, haven't they?

In Western nations there is an obsession with food. We eat to be sociable, to make ourselves feel good, for comfort, and many other reasons. There is a continual barrage of news about what is good and not good to eat. Up to that point of temptation, humans ate excellent things as part of the package, so to speak, of total goodness. Things tasted wonderfully and were enjoyed and eaten with gratitude. There was plenty, so there was no thought of any shortage. And there wouldn't be, would there, with the generous nature of the Creator? Food was a totally renewable resource occurring naturally with no work required to prepare. It was nutritious and abundant not only for humans, but for all living things.

Solomon observed, and we can agree, that the eye has no end of seeing. Can you see how devoted we are to what is pleasing to the eye? Since the twist was added to human experience we try to satisfy our minds, hearts and spirits with things that we see. From art, to porn, to styles of dress or decorating, to movies and magazines, to news shows and coffee table books we look and look and look. Before this temptation everything in the universe was very good. It was all beautiful, lovely, and wonderful. The people had perfect sight. Nothing was lacking. They saw everything alongside the great Creator. He satisfied them and they enjoyed this world with Him. Now we seek to fulfill ourselves apart from Him. But the eyes cannot be the port of entry for what will satisfy our spirits. Many have given testimony that once their spirits have been joined to Him, they see everything differently. That is truth, but we will get to that.

The desire to get ahead by knowing more is also an addictive trait in our world, isn't it? We are always learning, always making up new categories of information, always looking for the latest thing. New packaging on old ideas is enough to fool us into thinking there is something new. Again, Solomon had it right. "There is nothing new under the sun." Before the temptation, the people were perfectly intelligent. Their brains were very good. There was no lack of mental stimulation, and their intelligence was perfectly harmonious with the One who gave them minds and made the amazing universe it which they found themselves. There was plenty to know, and they were equipped to learn and delight in the One who made it all.

In this moment, though, the woman wanted wisdom apart from Him. Instead of brilliant understanding of the designs and laws that He put into the created order, she followed the tempter into an illusion of knowledge. The Bible says, "The fear of the Lord is the beginning of knowledge." Scripture does tell the truth. Information, facts, and details are not complete knowledge. We cannot really begin to know until we find that connection to Him again that was lost that day.

So she took the fruit and ate. She also gave some to her husband, who was with her, and he ate.

The knowledge of good AND evil was now in the world. The bait was swallowed. The temptation was complete. The fall had begun.

Discussion Questions

1. How do we react when we feel we are being gypped of something?

   How easy is it to persuade us that we are?

2. Can you see the roots of evil in all that makes life painful? Describe the connection.

Chapter Four

Consequence and Promise

I hate this part of reality. There are consequences in the real world. Satan succeeded in convincing the woman that there would be none, but he is a liar. In our world today we do things and hope there will be no consequence. We are fools to think that. We, like the first woman and man, are deceived.

We drink and hope for no hangover. We have sex with people we are not married to and hope for no STD and no baby and no broken heart. We fill our bodies with drugs of all sorts and hope for no side effects. We use credit to buy tons of things we do not wish to wait and save up for and hope that we will always be able to keep up on the payments, that we won't face bank-ruptcy. We verbally abuse the people closest to us and expect them to just roll with it.

The Creator put perfect order, beauty, and balance into the creation. It was very good in every sense of those words. The one rule was not a flaw. It was true. The knowledge of good *and* evil would bring immediate death. What the first people did not realize was the depth and breadth of that death. Nor did they realize the powerful, loving plan already in place for redeeming the pervasive consequences of their disobedience.

As soon as the man and woman ate the fruit, they knew they were naked. Until now they were unclothed and unashamed, beautiful and perfect. Suddenly the perfection was gone. Now there was fear and shame. They had to hide from each other! Welcome to the world of evil!

They tried to cover themselves with leaves from a fig tree as clothing. Then they heard the Lord God walking in the garden. This had always been a joyous time of sharing the events of the day and enjoying total contentment together, Creator and creatures. This time they hid themselves because they were afraid and ashamed.

Can you feel the loss here? We are so used to our own hiding, fear, shame, and alienation from God that we need to realize this was the first time any-thing like this was experienced in our world. Here is the first woman, perfect, relational, restful, beautiful, and enjoying from the time of her creation until now a safe, loving relationship with both her husband and the Creator of the universe. She disobeys and immediately wants to hide her vulnerability from her husband. Now she hides from the great Love of her life, the One who made her with intricate detail and who was pleased with her reflection of His image. In short her relationship with every other person became corrupted. There was no safe place for her anymore.

So the Lord calls to the man, "Where are you?" Interesting, isn't it, the One who had done nothing wrong initiates reconnection with the ones who broke the one rule? We have believed a lie about this great

God. We think He is watching for us to break a rule, to do something wrong, to mess up just so that He can smash us like a bug. We see Him as harsh, mean, inflexible, and angry. We are so very wrong.

The Lord God seeks the man. When He finds him, the man says they knew they were naked and so they hid themselves. Interesting. After all this time of perfect contentment in a world that was perfect for them, they now knew they had no clothing? No one else in the world had clothing either! It is interesting to discover something you didn't know existed is missing.

God saw through that, too. "Who told you you were naked?" God knew it was a person who had interfered. His question was not, "What makes you think that?" but "Who?" God had this enemy before the temptation. He used to be one of the closest, most beautiful angels around God's throne. His name had been Lucifer. But it entered his heart to not only be near to God and see His glory, Lucifer wanted to *be* God and receive the glory for himself. He coveted, was filled with pride, and came to loathe the God who made him. When he was cast down from Heaven, he took a third of the angels with him. God and he already had a history. So when the first people were messed up, God knew it was personal. His enemy wanted to destroy the work of His hands.

So begins the "Blame Game" that plagues our world from toddlers to politicians. It never happened before this conversation. The man, Adam, answers, "The woman You gave me—she gave me some of the fruit, and I ate it." Basically, he blamed everyone else in the world for his failure to keep his distance from the fruit. Notice, too, that the ones he had shared such perfect connection with were seen as the enemies.

The woman is questioned next. She passes the blame on, too. "The serpent deceived me and I ate." They both tell the truth, and they both avoid taking full responsibility for what they themselves did. This is one of the character-istics of the presence of evil. Evil diverts personal responsibility. To "come clean" is to simply admit your guilt. That is very hard for us to do, but no relationship can be fully restored without that. When we have been hurt, we don't want explanations, excuses, and certainly not accusations. We want our offender to just admit he/she hurt us and is sorry, that he/she was wrong.

So, the consequences, fair and just and merciful, are meted out. The serpent is now cursed above all the other creatures, will go about on its belly and eat dust every day of its existence. There would be enmity between the seed of the woman and the seed of the serpent perpetually. Eventually, the seed of the woman would crush the head of the serpent and the serpent would bruise his heel.

This is the first promise that Someone would be sent to deal with the enemy of God and people. He had so cunningly brought deception, which led to disobedience, which led to the presence of evil in this world. Someone born of woman's seed would enter in the future and defeat the serpent, crushing him. Indeed, One would come who would destroy the works of the devil.

The consequences go on. The woman would now have pain in childbearing. I believe that this is a truly pervasive curse. Women suffer from the whole childbearing system in their bodies, not just the act of bearing a child, which is in itself painful. PMS, menopause, cancers of various reproductive parts, cramps, bloating, and diseases of her delicately made body would now be a common part of woman's existence.

Her desire would be for her husband, but he would rule over her. The whole relationship is now going to be cockeyed. The depth of the meaning of this has yet to be thoroughly discovered and explained. We call some of this consequence "The Cinderella Complex." A woman tends to look for a man to give her what she used to receive directly from her Creator. She looks for a man that will make her feel secure, give her identity, a sense of belonging, a sense of being cared for, valued and loved. No matter how many times a woman has been hurt, divorced, or stung by a relationship, she will hope that the *next* man will be the "knight in shining armor," the strong, good one who will pursue and rescue her.

But a man is not going to simply exist to meet her needs. In fact, he will tend to be a harsh ruler over her, limiting and belittling her life. All over the world and down through the centuries, we see this cruelty to women from the mindsets of whole cultures. Women in Western cultures today probably have it better than women of any other subset, but still there is enough abuse to have fired off the suffragette movement and the women's liberation movement.

The presence of evil in this new world would infect the relationships between men and women down through the ages. Men and women would now find a mixed bag of experiences where once there had been a perfectly beautiful, free, happy companionable relationship between them to the great pleasure of their Creator. Every man and woman has felt the sting of this poisoning of relationship that once was very good.

The man's work became forever hard. Now there would be thorns and thistles. There would be laborious, sweaty work in order to get the plants to grow. He had once simply picked the food and eaten it. It would no longer be easy to keep body and soul together, so to speak. The "daily grind" would wear on him. It would now be difficult to make a living.

They did not die physically the day they ate, that would come; but everything became corrupted instantly. There was immediate separation. They made themselves enemies of God by believing lies about Him. They lost the life-giving connection with Him they had so freely enjoyed. They no longer would have a free and easy relationship with each other. Their connection to the created order would now be marred and the earth would not make it easy for them to live or eat.

Death physically would now become part of their lives, ending the forever lovely lives they would have had. Eventually soul and body would separate and their bodies would return to dust. Man was formed out of the earth and to earth his body would return. Physical death was on the way.

The man and woman were removed from the Garden. A guard was posted to keep them out so they would not be able to eat from the tree of life. It would not be good to live forever in their new evil state. God clothed them with animal skins to cover their nakedness. This was a picture of the coming salvation. The blood of an innocent would be shed to cover the guilt of wicked people.

Discussion Questions

1. Think about what was lost that day. Can you see the grace of the Creator in the terms of the Fall? Speak about some of those.

2. The most precious part of creation was now infected with the same evil that turned Lucifer against God. Do you think God felt that loss? Do you think He may have felt it more than Adam and Eve?

3. Do you think it is significant that God speaks of an eventual defeat of evil at this point of the story? Why? Can you see that He is still perfect and good? Talk about that.

Chapter Five

The Woman Looks for Help

So Adam names his wife Eve, which means mother of all the living. Their hope together is that she will produce a child who will defeat the deceiver.

They begin life again, outside the Garden of Eden this time. Contrary to popular beliefs that man is getting smarter, so, therefore, our ancestors were dumb and coarse, these were still the exquisite creatures that God had personally formed. They were flawed now relationally, but still highly intelligent and beautiful.

Adam now had to figure out how to get things to grow for food. Thorns and weeds now existed and made his work hard. He sweated with the exertion that was necessary to produce a crop. Eve could feel the difference in her relationships. Her husband no longer perfectly understood her. Her God was not visible and audible daily as He had been before. She knew loneliness.

She remembered the promise that a seed of woman would crush the serpent's head. So, when she had her firstborn son, she named him Cain saying, "With the help of the Lord I have brought forth a man." She had no idea the long years of human history that would be laid before the promise would be fulfilled. Let's see how her desire for her first son to be the one who would defeat the serpent worked out.

She had another son (among many sons and daughters) named Abel. Cain got into the farming and Abel got into raising cattle and sheep. Both sons were good at what they did. Adam instructed his sons in the worship of the God who made the world. He told them about the animals that were slain so the nakedness of their parents would be covered. He told them that blood would cover the sin so they could approach God in prayer. When the time for them to sacrifice on their own came, Cain offered up fruit from the soil. Abel offered fat portions from the firstborn of his flocks. Abel's offering was accepted by God, but Cain's was not.

The Lord God came to speak with Cain. The goodness of the Creator is again on display for all the human family to see. He pursued Cain. He did not have to, but like the mercy He showed in seeking Adam out after his dis-obedience, He has mercy again.

God instructed Cain that his offering would be accepted if he offered an appropriate one. His parents had tried coverings of fig leaves, but that was not acceptable. Blood must cover sin. God told him that sin was seeking to overcome Cain, but that Cain could be the victor if he would only do what was right.

Cain decided that what he brought should be accepted because it was he who brought it. He hated his brother for doing what was right, and murdered him.

The first physical death of a human was a violent one based on the hatred of evil for good. This violent hatred has marked human history ever since. Our stories are full of innocents who suffer at the hands of evil people from Cinderella and her step-mother and sisters to the genocides of today. Whole people groups have been slaughtered for no reason other than they were born into the "wrong" race or tribe. Innocent children are caught all the time in the consequences of their parents' choices to engage in evil. God was right about evil bringing death.

Eve, the mother of the murdered and the murderer, saw once again that the knowledge of good *and* evil came with a high price. Her hope that Cain would be the one who would defeat the serpent who deceived her was dashed to the ground. It would not be this "seed" who delivered.

Cain married one of his sisters (the genetics were not then infected with the defects that have multiplied over time) and became a "restless wanderer on the earth." The soil would no longer bear fruit for him. Interestingly he was afraid that whoever found him would kill him. I guess he knew the murder in his own heart could very well be in the hearts of his family members. So the good and gracious Creator God put a mark on him so that no one who found him would kill him. The mark somehow communicated that whoever killed Cain would suffer vengeance seven times over. Isn't the Lord merciful?

So Eve's firstborn is now wandering the earth. He is not the one who would fix this world. Her dear Abel is dead. Her heart knows great sorrow and grief. She then had another son, Seth, whom she saw as in the place of Abel since Cain had killed him. Her hope in the promise still lives. It is what keeps her going.

It is through the line of Seth that the Saviour eventually does come. The promise is not forgotten. It is preserved by the mighty and good Creator down through centuries. Seth's line does not die out until the promised Seed is born and plays His role in the human story.

Discussion Questions

1. Do we ever resent someone who does the right thing? Why do we not do the right thing?

2. Does it ever feel to us that other people have more favor with God? What do you think about God's talk with Cain? Could He be saying the same thing to us?

Chapter Six

God Sees and Knows

It is through the stories of others that we often find hope, help, courage, and truth. Even mundane issues like what to do with grass stain on jeans can be learned through a story of a friend.

I would like us to explore some stories of women since Eve's time so that we get a clearer picture of the similarities of distress that women face no matter their time on the planet, as well as, the great goodness of the Creator God. He breaks into the stories of women and displays great depth of under-standing, kindness, power, and love. We can respond in hope that He would be the One we need in our story every day.

Consider Hagar. She was an Egyptian woman who became a maidservant to Sarah (at this time she is still called Sarai), wife of Abraham (called Abram still at this point in his life). Abraham was a nomad with no permanent address, so Hagar traveled with the couple wherever they went serving the needs of her mistress, Sarah.

Now, God had told Abraham years before that He would make him the father of many nations, that his descendants would be as numerous as the stars in the sky and the sand on the seashore. The problem was that he did not have even one son yet and he was about 86 at this time.

So, Sarah reasons that God could use a little help. She goes to Abraham and says, "The Lord has kept me from having children. Go, sleep with my maidservant; perhaps I can build a family through her."

Hagar is a pawn in this strategy game. She is used by another woman without consultation in order to gain a child for that woman. I wish I could say that women are kind to their own gender, but that is still not true today. The Reader's Digest in 2010 carried an appalling story of a ring of *women* who through deceit enslaved a number of Guatemalan women for the sex trade in the United States, Los Angeles, I think.

The women's liberation movement has sought to sell the idea that it is men who dominate, humiliate, control, and stifle women. True as that may be they do not have a corner on that market. Women are cruel to other women: mothers to daughters, daughters to mothers, sisters to each other, etc. Women born into the fallen world are capable of great evil. The knowledge of evil has come at a high price to Eve's daughters.

Abram does not resist. He takes his wife's suggestion and sleeps with Hagar. She conceives. When she knew she was pregnant, she began to despise her mistress, Sarah. Can't you just see it? The old woman (about 76) hasn't been able to conceive after all these years. The young woman sleeps with the master and gets pregnant easily. She may be a maidservant, but she at least is fertile. Oh, the attitudes! Those are also tainted all around, aren't they? How many times do snippy, spiteful attitudes infect women's relation-ships! Even if what Sarah proposed was common among the peoples of her time, it still was a suggestion that gave Hagar the most intimate access to Abram, and vice versa.

By the way, I love the Bible from which this and many other rich stories come. One of the reasons I do is that stories such as this are not candy-coated to make Abraham and Sarah look better than they were. They became great heroes of the faith, great examples of those who trusted the God who created the world. Nevertheless, in this story Sarah is seen in living color and Abraham as pretty passive. We do not expect anything of Hagar, but the sweetest part of this story, the greatest lesson from this story is hers to tell.

Sarah picks up on the attitude shift in Hagar and complains to Abraham. He tells her that Hagar is her maidservant, "Do with her whatever you think best." So our heroine of the faith begins to mistreat Hagar so badly that Hagar flees from her.

I guess Sarah shows she has the upper hand. We are free to choose our way, but we are not free to choose the fallout from our choices. Sarah could simply have reasoned that God was able to make the universe out of nothing and could have waited for Him to fulfill the promise of a son in His own time in His own way. But she leaned on her own understanding after waiting for quite a while, came up with Plan B, and now showed her disrespectful pregnant handmaiden who was boss! Even women we would call "good" have their shameful moments, and this certainly was one of those in the life of Sarah.

Hagar, although she started the rift in the relationship, feels abused. She does not just flee. She flees from Sarah. It is personal, and it hurts. It gets so intense, so hopeless, so painful, and so personal that the only course that seems like any relief is to run alone out into the desert taking her chances out there.

Women suffer in relationships. They endure hardship of many kinds without complaint. Pioneer women certainly had it hard physically. Women in developing countries do their best to prepare what food they have and serve it to their families. During the Depression women found many creative ways to stretch meager provisions. They endure great pain in the bearing of children, but pain in relationship will take the heart right out of them.

Popular wisdom says a woman should stay in a relationally painful situation as long as there is no physical abuse. The excruciating pain of being verbally and emotionally abused makes a beating seem like nothing. Physical abuse never happens without the verbal and emotional damage, however, so maybe that is why the experts advise women the way they do.

Hagar ran to a spring beside a road. Now comes the great part. The angel of the Lord finds her there. This great God who created the world sends someone to find her. He asks her, "Hagar, slave of Sarai, where have you come from and where are you going?"

Please note that He knows her by name. Isn't that something? While He is writing a great story through the lives of Abraham and Sarah that will affect the world, He notices a slave girl in trouble and distress . . . by name!

I love that He asks where she has come from. So many times we women are shamed by our past, embarrassed by the treatment we have received from people who were supposed to love us, feeling that maybe we really are nothing of worth, not loveable, not good enough. God wants us to tell Him of our past. I and many women have found great peace by personally inviting God in to take a look at just how hard the worst things have been for her. When He enters those rooms of memory, things change like letting in fresh air does to a room long shut up full of stale air.

He also asks where she is going. That is a good question, too. When we are in a hopeless, hurtful circumstance, all we can think of is getting away from that; but we cannot see ahead. Where are we going? Where do we think we will find relief? The Lord God wants women to run to Him. He is our safe destination, the only safe place in a corrupt world. Anywhere else may look good until we arrive and stay a while. Even the most pleasant refuges apart from Him turn in time into prisons of their own . . . maybe worse than what we ran from. Where are we going?

The angel tells her that she is to return and submit to Sarah, that her son will be the first of so many descendants that they would be uncountable. He tells her, too, that he will be a fighter. Everyone's hand would be against him and his hand against everyone else. He would be tough, rugged like a wild donkey.

I am not sure those words would have been comforting to me. I would not like to see everyone fighting with my son, but what she got out of the encounter was hope. It was hope that went straight to her broken heart. She names the Lord God who spoke to her, "You are the God who sees me." She says, "I have now seen the One who sees me."

Do you know what this means? Above all the abuse, beyond the reach of defiant abusers is One who sees, One who cares. That makes all the difference. He is personal. He is taking note of her, of her life. She matters to Him, and He is huge, good, kind, and great in power. He knows the future. Her hope for her life and that of her son is now transferred totally over to this One who sees her. Someone is looking out for her, even if Sarai is still unreasonable. God is watching over her. She has seen Him. Her heart is quiet. She has changed.

From little kids at play, "Mommy watch!" to the importance of having a parent at ball games, graduations, and birthdays, it is life-giving to us humans to have someone notice us. It gives us value. It gives us hope. Hagar was able to go back into a situation that she did not know would be better and submit to the very person who had caused her such pain with a wonderful secret. There was One who saw her, who noticed her, and He was watching out for her and her son.

We see the untainted goodness of the Creator God in this story. He is not reaching out to a queen, but to a little slave. She is in need. She is in hopeless despair, but He finds her and speaks life into her. She is renewed and finds strength to do as He says knowing that He cares.

This is the only hope worthy of that name in this world for women anywhere. Nothing this confused and evil world offers as a refuge ultimately satisfies us in the deepest place of our being, the place from which we seek the answer to the question, "Am I loved?" The answer is from the heart of God Himself, "Yes, my dear girl, you are loved by the One who made you. Believe Me. I am worthy of your trust. Come home to my heart. You are safe with Me."

Discussion Questions

1. Have you ever had a bad attitude? Did it cause others to react to you in further bad attitudes? Did you feel like a victim of their abuse?

2. What would it mean to us to know there was someone who understood and would be watching out for our welfare? Can you feel the hope that would come from that kind of attention?

3. We can endure almost anything if we have hope. Can you think of any other stories of women who have endured by their hope in God?

Chapter Seven

God Announces to a Woman

In the ancient cultures any business was done through the man of the family. It is that way today in many cultures. Women are not allowed to own property, run a business officially, nor divorce their husbands. We women of western civilization find this unjust, unfair, wicked even. But for the women in those cultures, it is inescapable fact.

I have often wondered what God Himself, who created both man and woman must think of this seeming difference in importance between the genders. This story gives what I find a humorous view of the honor God shows women, as well as men. The story is from the 13th chapter of the book of Judges in the Bible.

> [2] A certain man of Zorah, named Manoah, from the clan of the Danites, had a wife who was childless, unable to give birth. We must break in here to explain that not being able to give birth was, and is still to a certain extent even in western culture, a devastating condition. Something is seriously wrong. Women are supposed to be able to

produce children. The heartache is real as month after month, year after year goes by with no baby. I do not know what the husbands feel about this, but I know that it is a deep grief to the women who are experiencing infertility. With just such a woman God breaks into her story. Listen. ³ The angel of the LORD appeared to her and said, "You are barren and childless, (pretty direct, huh?) but you are going to become pregnant and give birth to a son. (Wow! Out of the blue comes fantastic news! Not just a baby, but a valued son—important for carrying on the family name!) ⁴ Now see to it that you drink no wine or other fermented drink and that you do not eat anything unclean. ⁵ You will become pregnant and have a son whose head is never to be touched by a razor because the boy is to be a Nazirite, dedicated to God from the womb. He will take the lead in delivering Israel from the hands of the Philistines."

These instructions seem a little strange, but the Philistines were harassing the Israelites greatly. To think that the deliverance would begin through this baby boy was welcome news. Such news was worth even the odd restrictions on diet and the fact that her son was to have long hair and a beard (when he got old enough). The instructions for Nazirite vows were spelled out by Moses in the law years, maybe centuries before this story. We are not sure how often a man would take them up, but there was at least a distant memory for this woman of a special "set-apartness" of this man to God his whole life beginning now before he was even conceived.

> ⁶ Then the woman went to her husband and told him, "A man of God came to me. He looked like an angel of God, very awesome. I didn't ask him where he came from, and he didn't tell me his name. ⁷ But he said to me, 'You will become pregnant and have a son. Now then, drink no wine or other fermented drink and do not eat anything unclean, because the boy will be a Nazirite of God from the womb until the day of his death.'"

I love the simplicity and openness of her relationship to her husband. She tells him the unusual events of her day straight out. I love also the description of the angel, "very awesome." She probably had been running the story through her head all the way over to where she found her husband. Lots of facts are missing: his name, where he came from, why she was chosen, etc. She decided to just tell what she knew. The most important facts were there: she was to restrict her diet, she would conceive a son, and he would begin to deliver from the Philistines. Interestingly, she did not relate that last fact. Was it too much?

> ⁸ Then Manoah prayed to the LORD: "Pardon your servant, Lord. I beg you to let the man of God you sent to us come again to teach us how to bring up the boy who is to be born."

This is sweet to me. The husband goes to the Lord, on his own, to ask for directions. I love that! We have jokes about how hard this is for men to do generally, but this man did. Some may feel he is trying to break into the conversation between God and his wife, but he seems humble and sincere.

> [9] God heard Manoah, and the angel of God came again to the woman while she was out in the field; but her husband Manoah was not with her. [10] The woman hurried to tell her husband, "He's here! The man who appeared to me the other day!"

This is definitely making a point. The angel comes again to the woman! What is that? I think it is an honoring of her worth, her importance, her value in God's eyes. He is not seeing her as second class, as a baby factory, as anything degrading. God is honoring *her* with another visit as answer to *her husband's* prayer! I am not sure how man-dominated cultures would see this, but I am pretty sure that it might be left out of the narrative. Isn't it just lovely that God does this? Can you not feel the gracious honor this gives to this unnamed barren wife? She matters. God sees her as capable of understanding. He chooses to honor her, to give her hope, to soothe the years of bitter disappointment.

I love, too, that she is not in any way trying to exclude her husband. She is loving, gracious, and kind in hurrying to bring her husband in on this second visit. She has a sharing, generous spirit. She is not trying to keep him "out of the loop," so to speak.

> [11] Manoah got up and followed his wife. When he came to the man, he said, "Are you the man who talked to my wife?"
>
> "I am," he said.

Can you not just see this encounter? The husband verifies the stranger. The awesome angel of the Lord is confronted by a simple Israelite farmer.

> [12] So Manoah asked him, "When your words are fulfilled, what is to be the rule that governs the boy's life and work?"

This is a fair question from the dad-to-be. After all, with this kind of introduction this baby boy must be unusual. "How are we to train him?" seems a fair inquiry.

> [13] The angel of the LORD answered, "Your wife must do all that I have told her. [14] She must not eat anything that comes from the grapevine, nor drink any wine or other fermented drink nor eat anything unclean. She must do everything I have commanded her."

Again with the honoring of the wife! No further instructions are forthcoming. The man is not going to get a fuller report. She has been told. She understands. She has the instructions that are complete enough. Notice, too, the personal nature of the comment, "everything I have commanded her." I do not think it was/is common for another man to command someone else's wife. It is as though he claims His own connection to her. I believe that is what this is about. Maybe it is simply to give encouragement to all women who feel less than valued by their culture that they are welcomed by God Himself to have their own direct connection to Him. They do not have to go through their husbands or anyone else to reach the God who created both male and female. Isn't that wonderful news?! Remember at the beginning both Adam and Eve had personal connections to the Lord God who made them. This seems to be an invitation to resume that individual connection.

> [15] Manoah said to the angel of the LORD, "We would like you to stay until we prepare a young goat for you."

Hospitality and, perhaps, he is hoping to get a better read on this "awesome" visitor.

> [16] The angel of the LORD replied, "Even though you detain me, I will not eat any of your food. But if you prepare a burnt offering, offer it to the LORD." (Manoah did not realize that it was the angel of the LORD.)

This visitor has very clear parameters. He is not here for a social visit. He is all about what the Lord God is doing. The whole thing is God's thing. There is no horizontal dimension to this. This is a vertical God encounter. God is breaking in to the history of not only this couple, but the Jewish nation. Oh, the stories that will be told of this boy! The Philistines are about to get a "heads up" that they are not the biggest power in the land. This baby boy will "bring it!"

> [17] Then Manoah inquired of the angel of the LORD, "What is your name, so that we may honor you when your word comes true?"

This was one of the details that had been missing since the first encounter. He tries to plug that hole at least.

> [18] He replied, "Why do you ask my name? It is beyond understanding." Don't you just love the dignity of that answer? God is so fantastically good, so wonderful, so beyond any greatness we could imagine that His Name itself

is beyond understanding. Wow! [19] Then Manoah took a young goat, together with the grain offering, and sacrificed it on a rock to the LORD. And the LORD did an amazing thing while Manoah and his wife watched: [20] As the flame blazed up from the altar toward heaven, the angel of the LORD ascended in the flame. Seeing this, Manoah and his wife fell with their faces to the ground. [21] When the angel of the LORD did not show himself again to Manoah and his wife, Manoah realized that it was the angel of the LORD.

The woman had a sense from the start that this was a man of God "like an angel of the Lord", but with his analytical mind, the man now concurs and sees the inherent danger of such a reality.

[22] "We are doomed to die!" he said to his wife. "We have seen God!"

[23] But his wife answered, "If the LORD had meant to kill us, he would not have accepted a burnt offering and grain offering from our hands, nor shown us all these things or now told us this."

Hers is a voice of relational reason. She gets it. She is in awe of Him, but knows that harm to them is not in the picture. I think she has just met her Hero and has had her evaluation of herself renovated. She has encountered the wonderful God from of old, and loves Him. She feels perfectly safe, though clearly in awe still.

This revelation sets women free to live their lives noticed, loved, valued, honored, cared for, and seen by their Creator. The God who made woman has not lost His delight in her no matter how unimportant the world may see her to be.

> [24] The woman gave birth to a boy and named him Samson. He grew and the LORD blessed him, [25] and the Spirit of the LORD began to stir him . . .

The exploits of her magnificent son over 20 years of his adult life are yours for the reading. No one else in the history of man has done the creative, strength-requiring, and sometimes humorous things he did. He stands unique to this day. At the end of his life, we see that his brothers came to bury him. (Judges 16:31) So this dear lady had other children as well. He was the first son born from her womb, and he did wonderful, unexpected things; but he was not the last that God enabled her to bear. She bore other sons, too. God took good care of her all her days. Isn't He a wonderful, personal God?

Discussion Questions

1. Have you or anyone else you know ever struggled with infertility? Describe the feelings of that trial.

2. Do you see in the world's religions a preference for the male followers of that religion? Give some examples.

3. From this story do you think that God holds the same view?

4. What does it mean to you that God Himself welcomes you, a woman, into relationship directly with Him?

Chapter Eight

Nabal and Abigail

The people a woman lives with, works with, or is related to, are capable of causing her great pain. It is my observation that women suffer most deeply in relationships. Some women have learned to harden themselves so well that no one could picture them relating to anyone. If you dig a little deeper, you will find that the pain of their past has led them to put up defenses around their hearts to protect themselves. If the people who were supposed to love them did not express that unconditional love, the wounded girl begins to compensate in one way or another. Women are born with great relational capacity. They hunger all their lives, no matter who they are or what defenses they use, for genuine love and real friendship.

Our lady in this story had an especially hard case. She was married to a fool. In fact his name, Nabal, means "fool." We will take some time looking at this fact, so that we may get some insight into the pressures in her life. The Bible has a lot to say about wise and foolish people. Back in the mid-60's Jan Silvious wrote a book called *Fool-proofing*

Your Life. If this chapter rings a loud bell about your own life, I would highly recommend the book. It is clear, Biblical, and helpful.

Fools see themselves as always right. No one could tell Nabal anything. He did not acknowledge any ideas that were not his initially. No matter what the fool does, says, or thinks it is inherently right. There is no other consideration to be given. The fool defines "rightness" by his own person. "If I think it, feel it, say it, perceive it; then it is right. No one is going to tell me differently."

You may be able to see why this person would be a relational nightmare. Healthy relationships involve a great deal of listening and understanding of the other person's point of view. It involves being understood as well. The fool cannot engage in the first activity since he is self-contained, as well as always right. There is no desire to mess up his mind with the thoughts and perspectives of other people. As far as being understood is concerned, he does not explain. He may even get hostile and abusive when asked to explain where he is coming from when he makes his sweeping judgments of the world as he sees it. He does not want understanding as much as he wants to be seen and honored as right. He is fine as king in a world of his own making.

The people in his life are not allowed into the inner workings of his thoughts. That would be too threatening. They might find some false assumptions, or faulty logic. In fact it may seem to a fool that people are always making him seem like he is wrong. He will not tolerate that. "Why am I always the bad guy?"

A fool is deceitful. He will go to great lengths to manipulate others by projecting an image that he deems acceptable to the world at large, never allowing the ones out there in the business world or larger social network to see the private hell in which he keeps his closest associates. He may be smooth and charming, humorous, capable, and competent in many areas. He will use that veneer to throw people "off the scent" so to speak. "If I am abusive, how is it that I am so popular, successful, efficient, etc." He deludes himself on every side into thinking he alone is right, no one else is necessary. In fact, it is the job of everyone else to shore up his inflated opinion of his own opinions. Let anyone question the validity of his perspective and a cocktail of abusive, belittling, scornful, and hurtful words will ensue.

He likes the world according to himself. He plays the innocent victim in all his stories. He is the hero in his world. Everyone else plays a supporting role to shore up his image of himself. He is complacent. This arrangement works well for him. There is no need to change anything. He bears no fault for anything in his life. The fault is clearly anyone and everyone else's. The Bible says of Nabal that he was "so surly no one could speak to him." He and other fools simply will not acknowledge any truth outside themselves.

Abigail is not alone with this predicament. Husbands are not the only fools in the world, either. Many women are fools, and a foolish wife or mother is no picnic either. Let's see how Abigail's story unfolds now that we have some of the setting.

Discussion Questions

1. Have you ever lived or worked with someone who was never wrong in his/her own eyes? What was that like? How did you cope?

2. How important is it to human relationships that we admit our own guilt or fault in offenses? What are some things that help us to see our fault?

3. How realistic is it to imagine that we are faultless? What is a better mindset?

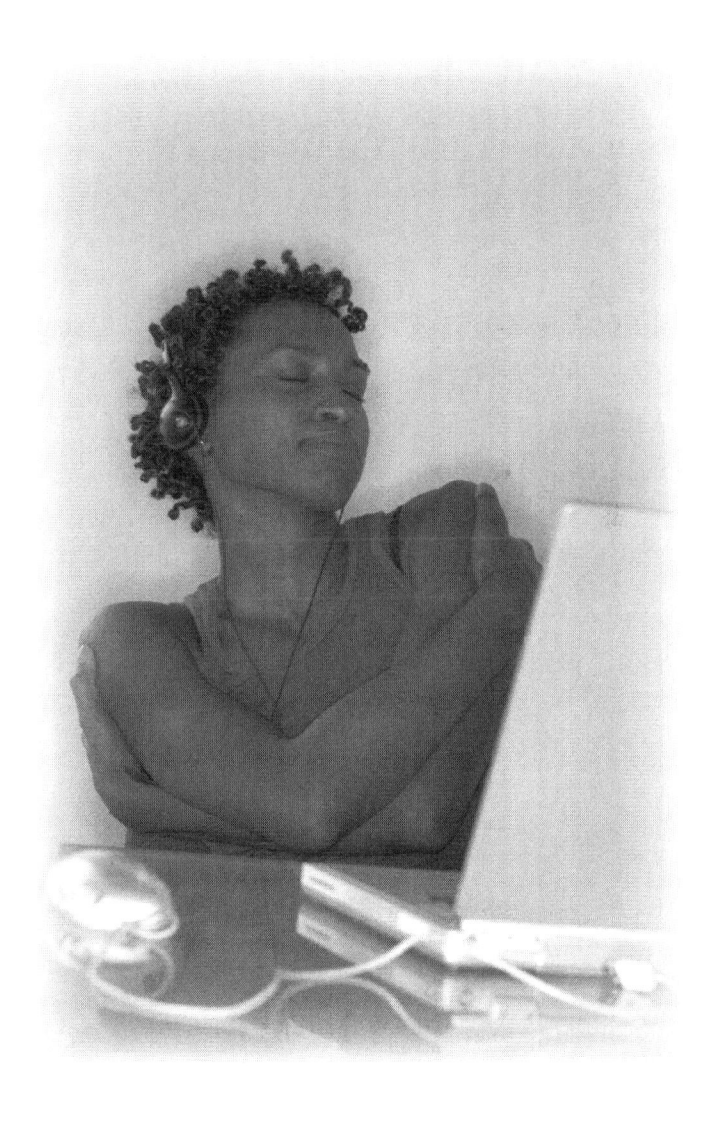

Chapter Nine

Nabal and Abigail Part 2

Abigail was married, as we said in the last chapter, to Nabal, whose name means Fool. How she got in that predicament we are not told. Perhaps it was an arranged marriage. Her parents might have been especially concerned that she marry a wealthy man so that she would never lack for anything. Nabal was rich. Or perhaps his charm could be turned on and sustained for the time of courting and he won her heart, only to be turned decidedly off as soon as they were married and she was caught. Like the trophy stuffed heads of game mounted in a man's lodge, once she was his no more attention was given to her. Her role was to make his life work. Whatever happened to join this beautiful and intelligent woman to this fool, the fact remained she was his wife.

We will see which of the ways she chose to deal with living with her fool in this story. What kind of woman did she become after seeing in living color day after day what kind of man she had married? The marriage was permanent, until death of one of the partners. She could have felt trapped. She probably did. As his words and behavior belittled her and everyone around her except for business guests who came to buy some of his wealth of sheep or goats, she could have been tempted to shrink into herself and erase who she really was. It was only too clear that he thought nothing of her. He only cared that she played her role in his world.

The historical setting for this story matters as well. Israel had settled into the Promised Land years ago. The various tribes had taken portions of the rich lands and conquered them with the help of the God who had promised the land to Abraham centuries before. The Hebrew people had looked around to the nations they displaced and the ones who were still their neighbors and discovered something they wanted. They wanted a king so they could be like everyone else. Not really a good motivation since the Lord God had led them by miracles and wonders out of the land of slavery, Egypt, and through the wilderness, feeding them miraculously every day, and into the land of promise. Even there He was faithful to guide their battle plans and give them success. After they conquered some of the land, they lost interest in taking it all and wandered from faith in the only God who ever did anything for people. They settled for worshiping gods of fertility, harvest, and power. They became prey for other nations to oppress. Then God would send one judge after another to rescue them. (Samson was one of those.) They would stay with the Lord for a while and then fall away again. So now they wanted a king. And God gave them Saul.

Saul began his reign with humility. He was head and shoulders taller than the other men of the kingdom, but he was more aware of all the ways in which he did not qualify to serve as king. He was from the tribe of the youngest son of Jacob. He was the youngest son in his family. He did not feel noble, or strong, or like he deserved to be chosen as king. Isn't that refreshing?

Unfortunately, he did not apparently believe the stories of God taking nobodies and making them really something. There were lots of them in the nation of Israel. This God was mighty and good, but Saul had not learned to love or trust Him beyond maybe a surface idea of who He was. After several episodes of disobedience, God said enough; and had David, the youngest son of a man of the tribe of Judah, anointed king.

David was a young man of great faith. He was a shepherd by profession. He took his job seriously rescuing his father's sheep from the paw of a lion and a bear with only his slingshot. He had a great heart for the sheep under his care and counted on God to help him fulfill his responsibilities to them. It is amazing the training God counts as useful in making His great people. In making a king we send them to the best tutors, train them in battle strategies and political histories, teach them to fight and ride. God sees the "transferable skills" of the shepherd. Moses was a shepherd for forty years before God had him lead His people out of Egypt and across the desert to a new "pasture." David was a man who loved and listened to the Lord God. He was a poet, a musician, a brave fighter, and a good friend.

But he was anointed king while Saul was still alive and ruling. The main enemy of Israel at that time was the Philistine nation. David slew their champion, Goliath, when he was still young. He became a popular commander of the Hebrew warriors. He was best friends with the king's son. And King Saul became afraid of the favor of God and of people that rested on David. When kings become afraid of a person, they seek to destroy him. David spent years fleeing from Saul and fighting Philistines as he went. He had a loyal, fierce group of men with him as he fled and fought. Saul had been within easy reach of David twice. David could easily have ended his life, and his men wanted him to; but he said he would not raise his hand against the one anointed by God as king. If God wanted him to be king, He would remove Saul without David's help. So Saul was David's enemy for the rest of Saul's life, but David was not Saul's enemy. It was during this time that David and his men settled for a time in the same area as Abigail was living day after day with her fool.

It is interesting, don't you think, how life can be going on seemingly the same day after day and then can radically change with one unforeseen event? So it was with our dear Abby. It was sheep shearing time in spring. Winter was over. The sheep were fat with wool. It was a celebration time every year, lots of food after each day of harvesting the thick valuable fiber from the animals. Generosity usually flowed. It was not unusual to invite travelers to join in the party, so great was the time!

So Abigail was busy this day thinking it was another day of making sure there was plenty to eat and that everyone was seen to. There was grain to roast, bread to bake, sheep to roast, cakes of raisins and figs to make, wine to serve.

She was busy overseeing all this happy activity when a servant of the household came to her with alarming news. He said that David had sent messengers to Nabal to ask to be part of the celebration, to share in some of the abundant food. Remember David had grown up around sheep and knew the hospitality of this time of year. His request was not out of line. The servant went on to tell Abigail that for some time David and his men had been in the country where Nabal's flocks were pastured. David's men had been like an impenetrable wall around the sheep. They protected them from natural predators and did not take any of them for themselves all the time out there. Nabal's shepherds were not harmed either. No harm had come to any of them, and great protection from these strong men was given. Anyone in his right mind would have invited the whole group down to join in the festivities with open heart of gratitude for the service they had given. Much was owed to them.

But Nabal had insulted and belittled David and his men with his answer. He said, "Who is this David? Who is this son of Jesse? Many servants are breaking away from their masters these days. Why should I take my bread and water, and the meat I have slaughtered for my shearers, and give it to men coming from who knows where?" Not only does he not give the hospitality that the culture of that area is still famous for, but he makes David out to be a runaway servant of no merit. David, who has been a champion of Israel, powerful in battle, anointed of God to be the next king, and a man of great integrity is treated like a naughty little boy deserving of no respect! He speaks of David's men as a troop of low-lives from nowhere, never mind that those same men have greatly benefited him by protecting his property so well that nothing was missing for the whole time they were out there. The shepherds knew they were there and were grateful that the men's strength was not used against them. Nabal showed no sense in his insulting, arrogant answer.

The servant got it. "Now think it over and see what you can do, because disaster is hanging over our master and his whole household. He is such a wicked man that no one can talk to him." The warriors in the hills would be sweeping down to wipe out every male on the whole ranch. There would be no more "Nabal's Acres."

It has been said that character is made in the quiet places where a person is alone with his thoughts, but it is revealed in crises. Such it was with Abigail. If over the years full of days with her tortuous fool she had become vindictive, bitter, resentful, and unforgiving, she would have run out to place signs, "This way to Nabal." If she had responded by becoming a fool herself caught up completely in constantly claiming her own rights, she would have missed the importance of this message. But she had for years full of days decided to trust herself to the Lord God of Israel. She had forged a deep faith in Him, an understanding of His ways, and a wisdom that comes only by seeking His mind in a world where others may not. She set her heart to know Him even while day after day she experienced the lack of love and wisdom in her husband. She determined long since to become the woman God intended His created ones to be no matter what anyone else chose. And she became quite a woman.

She flew into thoughtful, purposeful action. She and her servants loaded up a string of donkeys with every type of delicious food that had been prepared for the feast and sent the servants with the donkeys ahead of her right into the hills to head off the coming wave of destruction. She was coming right behind them pulling words from her deep well of understanding and wisdom. The men she was going to face were set to kill. They were warriors of honor, brave, loyal, and incensed by the arrogance of her husband's answer. How can one woman turn that kind of tide of manly rage?

> As she came riding her donkey into a mountain ravine, there were David and his men descending toward her, and she met them. [21] David had just said, "It's been useless—all my watching over this fellow's property in the wilderness so that nothing of his was missing. He has paid me back evil for good. [22] May God deal with David, be it ever so severely, if by morning I leave alive one male of all who belong to him!"

²³ When Abigail saw David, she quickly got off her donkey and bowed down before David with her face to the ground. ²⁴ She fell at his feet and said: "Pardon your servant, my lord, and let me speak to you; hear what your servant has to say. ²⁵ Please pay no attention, my lord, to that wicked man Nabal. He is just like his name—his name means Fool, and folly goes with him. And as for me, your servant, I did not see the men my lord sent. ²⁶ And now, my lord, as surely as the LORD your God lives and as you live, since the LORD has kept you from bloodshed and from avenging yourself with your own hands, may your enemies and all who are intent on harming my lord be like Nabal. ²⁷ And let this gift, which your servant has brought to my lord, be given to the men who follow you.

²⁸ "Please forgive your servant's presumption. The LORD your God will certainly make a lasting dynasty for my lord, because you fight the LORD's battles, and no wrongdoing will be found in you as long as you live. ²⁹ Even though someone is pursuing you to take your life, the life of my lord will be bound securely in the bundle of the living by the LORD your God, but the lives of your enemies he will hurl away as from the pocket of a sling. ³⁰ When the LORD has fulfilled for my lord every good thing he promised concerning him and has appointed him ruler over Israel, ³¹ my lord will not have on his conscience the staggering burden of needless bloodshed or of having avenged himself. And when the LORD your God has brought my lord success, remember your servant."

In a few well chosen words she acknowledges the heart of the crisis, takes the blame on herself, reminds David of his noble heart and certain future, and appeals to his intimate reliance on God to establish the kingdom in his hands when the time is right. She honors the one who honors the Lord and does not want him sidetracked from his faith and integrity by a stupid fool. Avenging himself would not be in keeping with his life so far. There were innocent men down there who were not responsible for Nabal's foolishness. Her whole heart yearns to see the Lord honored in how this tragedy is avoided.

With the testosterone levels elevated like this she could not have been sure of her success in protecting the lives of her fool and their servants, but she gave all she had out of the recesses of her noble, faith-filled heart. She herself lived by this same faith she saw in David. Hers was as impossible a situation as his. Both were under the rule of one who wanted them out of the way. Saul wanted David dead. Nabal wanted her to be reduced to being absorbed into his self-centered worldview with no interest in anything she was apart from the role he had assigned her in "his world." She had chosen to trust the Lord God with her very life, her destiny, her influence. She had chosen to believe that to God she mattered, that He saw her daily acts of love and service to her husband and the others of the household, and that He was pleased with her. She saw in David the same determination to trust God in the face of his enemy and do what was right in the eyes of God no matter how hard it might be. She wanted him to run the race by God's rules so that he would win fairly and with no regrets.

Can you feel the power of this woman's influence? David was no minor character in the nation's life at that time. Here he is by some twist of circumstance in her backyard ready to eliminate the keeper of her prison, and she sees only the need to honor the holy, right, powerful God they both believe in.

The crisis is averted. Her words have found their mark and bring life. David says,

> "Praise be to the LORD, the God of Israel, who has sent you today to meet me. [33] May you be blessed for your good judgment and for keeping me from bloodshed this day and from avenging myself with my own hands. [34] Otherwise, as surely as the LORD, the God of Israel, lives, who has kept me from harming you, if you had not come quickly to meet me, not one male belonging to Nabal would have been left alive by daybreak."

He accepts the gifts of food from her hand and sends her home in peace. He has heard her words and granted her request to turn aside from revenge and let God settle the score.

Can you imagine the servants' view of their mistress on the way back down to the ranch? Wow! What courage, what insight, what wisdom, what strength!

So she gets home and Nabal is feasting like a king and so drunk she decides to wait until morning to tell him of the averted crisis, which he had created by his surly, mean words. In the morning she tells him all. His heart fails him and he slips into a coma and ten days later the Lord "struck Nabal and he died."

David hears news of this and says, "Praise be to the LORD, who has upheld my cause against Nabal for treating me with contempt. He has kept his servant from doing wrong and has brought Nabal's wrongdoing down on his own head."

Both David and Abigail are set free. David sends for Abby to take her as his wife. She and her five female servants go to a new life ready to serve the ones who have gathered around David in support until he becomes Israel's second king.

The Creator God was accessible to this woman in a difficult marriage from the moment she realized she was in trouble. He gave her wisdom, courage, and strength. He sustained her life day after day. He looked after her and kept her heart pure and safe even while she was in the home of a fool. He delivered her and made her a queen. She trusted Him and was not disappointed.

Discussion Questions

1. What do we do when we find ourselves in an impossible situation at work, at home, with family or in a neighborhood? Besides turning to the Lord for help, what do we do?

2. What would it take on a daily basis to do what Abigail did? What would that look like? Feel like?

3. Can you see how God's ways are better than our ways? Discuss how much better both in Abigail's life and in your own or someone you know.

Chapter Ten

THE PROMISED SEED

Remember the promise that a seed of woman would crush the head of the seed of the serpent? This promise was given immediately after the disobedience of the human pair. God was not going to let His enemy simply ruin the whole picture without revealing that there already was a plan in place to bring His precious people back to Himself.

For long centuries after Adam and Eve, people had the choice to love God the Creator and believe Him. God intervened at times into human history as we have seen in the stories we have looked at. People were never totally without evidence that the good God who made everything was still good, powerful, loving, kind, and active in the world. I am told that in pagan cultures all over the world there is a god in their various systems of belief who is good. They say, "We don't worry about him." Their entire system is set up on fear of the gods that are not so nice. Appeasing them is the basis of their religion.

God chose a people group for Himself. Through them He chose to display a foreshadowing of the Way back to Him. He chose Abraham, his son Isaac, his son Jacob, his twelve sons, and the descendants from them. Coming out of bondage in Egypt they became the nation of Israel (a second name for Jacob). To them and for the sake of the whole world God made known His design for true human behavior in the Ten Commandments. He also gave them a beautiful system of sacrifices that allowed the blood of an innocent animal to pay for the sin of a person. This was not the guess work system of appeasing pagan gods. This was the word of the Creator Himself revealing to the world the rescue plan was under way. Help was coming!

Promises about that Seed were clarified to the nation of Israel through their prophets. He would come from the line of Abraham, Isaac, Jacob, Judah, and David (the same one who married Abigail). He would be born of a virgin. He would be born in Bethlehem in Judah. He would be gentle, caring. He would be a healer and deliverer from the enemy. He would be the ultimate innocent sacrifice for anyone in the whole world who would believe. He paid for the removal of sin with his own blood. If sin is removed, relationship is opened between the Creator and His creatures. Promise was also made that the same Spirit of God that would empower this Seed in His life here would be in His followers also. He would empower them to know God the Creator and live the kind of lives that humans were designed to live.

This Seed has come. I want us to see how different He was from the forceful, push-people-out-of-the-way-to-get-what-I-want kind of conquerors the world has seen so many of. He is altogether good, and He came for us.

The last prophet of Israel had written 400 years prior. It was a long time since direct word had come from God to the people He had chosen.

There were many who still told the stories and knew what the prophets had said. They were looking for the One spoken about to rescue the world from the infectious curse of sin and all its consequences in the world.

One of those who knew and looked forward to the deliverance from the evil one was a young girl of the line of David in the tribe of Judah. An angel appeared to her to tell her that she was highly favored of God, that God was with her, and that she would bear a son who would save His people from their sins. She was to call His name Jesus. Hers had been a normal life up to that day. She did not seem to be anything special. But as the virgin through whom God's own Son would come, she was dear to God Himself.

The angel kindly told her of a relative of hers who also was pregnant after she had been barren her whole married life and was thought to be past the age of child-bearing. So, young Mary went to visit Elizabeth who was six months along in her pregnancy. Her son was also announced by an angelic visit. Gabriel had appeared to her husband, a priest, while he was serving in the temple. This baby was to announce the coming of Mary's baby preparing the way for people to believe Him.

Do you not see the kindness and understanding of God in this historical event? He knows women. He made them. It was now time for this amazing plan for the salvation of the whole world to be unfolded. His own Son was coming into the world. God chose the most upside down way, as He seems to do often, for the huge rescue in mind to happen; and He takes care of all the relational details for the women involved.

Mary was most likely a teenage girl at the time. Who was going to believe an unwed teen was divinely impregnated? Her dear elderly relative so wondrously had conceived herself would be a great resource of encouragement, stability, and reinforcement. It is OK to believe God!

I can imagine in the three months that young Mary was there the two of them would talk freely about the divine intervention of God into their lives. Elizabeth's husband was actually struck dumb until after the birth of their son John because he did not believe the angel, so the two women talked to their hearts' content. I imagine that he enjoyed listening to them at mealtimes, even though he could not join in the verbal conversation. God provided the two women for each other just as surely as He provided their sons for world-changing roles. God covers all the bases, so to speak. He is wonderful in knowledge, wisdom, and great understanding.

Discussion Questions

1. We are so used to the happy Christmas story that we may not have really given much thought to how it felt to be Mary. Think of a teen girl you know. What would be some of her concern if she were given such a message?

2. Has another woman ever been a source of comfort and strength to you? What were the circumstances? How did she help?

3. Read in Luke 1:39-56 the interaction between Elizabeth and Mary, and Mary's song. What kind of faith does it appear they have? How did that happen?

Chapter Eleven

The Seed in Early Life

So the One sent to undo, destroy, and reverse the works of evil in the world comes to us in the form of a baby born to a couple from a small out-of-the-way town called Nazareth. The announcement by angels of His birth was made to shepherds outside the town of Bethlehem, where His parents had gone to be taxed by command of the Romans. Shepherds were almost at the bottom of the social hierarchy in Israel. I do not know how that happened. Moses and David, as we have mentioned, both came to lead Israel from shepherding. Nevertheless, shepherds were, at the time Jesus was born, considered so worthless they could not even testify in court.

Do you see the heart of the Creator? Jesus is the Way for humans to come back to friendship with God. It does not matter how steeped in the evil of the world, how abused by the evil of others, how unimportant the people may seem to their own culture. Jesus was sent to this corrupt, lost, fallen, polluted world to bring an invitation of restoration to the Father who has always loved His creation, always provided the order in the universe: rain, sunrises, sunsets, seasons, and crops. The Father has not abandoned His creation. He has always been calling through His Word, His prophets, and the awesome beauty and intricacy of His world to humans, "Come find Me. This world is not all there is. You are loved. I love you." Now at just the right time for the relationship to be restored the Father sends Jesus into the Roman Empire controlled land of the Jews. He has come to be the Savior of the entire world.

He does not come with great fanfare to a royal palace somewhere. He is not invading the world with a conquering army. He comes where anyone could approach him. The shepherds did the night He was born. Maybe they were almost worthless in the eyes of their culture, but God wanted them to be the first to know that the Lamb of God was born. Lambs through the centuries since the Law was given were frequent sacrifices for sin in Israel. They had to be male, first-born of their mommy ewes, without spot or blemish, and young adults of a year old. Who better to know of the birth of a lamb than shepherds? They went, sought, and found in the town the things the angel told them about. They told Mary and Joseph what had happened to them, and then they told everyone else. People were amazed that shepherds had so much to say and the bold excitement with which they told the wonder-filled events of the dark night on the hills outside Bethlehem. What a fantastic story!

But God also loves the rich and wise. So He puts a star in the sky that men from the Far East notice. They search through their ancient writings (without the aid of Google, I might add) and find a prophecy made by an ancient seer from Midian about the future Israelite ruler. The seer's name was Balaam. Numbers 22-24 tells the story of how this pagan diviner was used to bring one unusual prophecy concerning the coming King of kings. The wise men of the East read,

"I see him, but not now;

I behold him, but not near.

A star will come out of Jacob; a scepter will rise out of Israel."

So they prepare royal gifts of gold, frankincense and myrrh to bring to the newborn. It takes some time to get there traveling across the miles without the modern conveniences of train, cars or buses. By the time they get to Israel ready to worship this long prophesied baby, he is a young child. The family is in a house, probably back in Nazareth. They present their gifts along with their story and their worship. From the least important to the highly honored, the invitation includes all of mankind before baby Jesus does anything. The Father-Creator is welcoming people back to the great, loving friendship and safety of His heart.

The evil one who has been enjoying his torture, torment and deception of humans since the Garden of Eden is alerted by the visit of the Wise Men. They had come to the palace in Jerusalem looking for this One born King of the Jews, the name which eventually Pilate has written on the sign above Jesus on the cross. Problem is the Romans are in charge and Herod is king. He is so insecure and dangerous that history tells us he had a number of his own family killed to secure his unchallenged right to rule. Jewish scholars are summoned to answer where the King was to be born. They came back with the answer from the prophet Micah,

"But you, Bethlehem Ephrathah, though you are small among the clans of Judah, out of you will come for me one who will be ruler over Israel, whose origins are from of old, from ancient times."

The wise men go on their way with that answer, see the star over the house where the child Jesus was, present their worship and gifts, and are warned in a dream not to go back to Herod, who had asked them to report back. After some time Herod gets nervous about this delay. So Herod, with a little help from the evil one, gives the order for every boy from newborn to two years old to be slaughtered in order to kill the competition. The seed of the serpent will not concede. He influences human agents to try to wipe the seed of woman off the face of the planet. He evidently did not know who Jesus was from the angelic visit, or perhaps he needed high officials to give the order and human agents to carry out the summons. Either way, before Jesus is very old he has some powerful enemies.

God again sends Joseph a dream. Its message, "Get up. Take Mary and Jesus and flee to Egypt and stay there until I tell you it is safe to come back. Herod is going to search for the child to kill him." Joseph wasted no time. He knew what neurotic violence Herod was capable of. They left that night. So the Father protected His Son through Joseph. Joseph, the human guardian of Jesus, listened to and obeyed the real Father all the way. Between the two of them, Jesus grew up nice and healthy and strong.

By the way, Jewish prophets had foretold the grief of the mothers whose baby boys were slaughtered in the rush to eliminate Jesus, and the flight into Egypt. Hundreds of prophecies were fulfilled in the life of Jesus, not because Jesus studied and made them happen. The ones we have referred to so far were completely out of a baby's ability to make happen. Over three hundred prophecies were fulfilled by Jesus in His lifetime on earth. They were fulfilled because God the Father sees everything, planned everything centuries ahead, and called them all into existence at just the right time for each. This should be comforting to us. Even though the enemy has us thinking that the world is an evil place, it truly is still God's own created world. He ultimately calls the shots. Jesus came to destroy the works of the enemy, and that is just what He would do according to the plan established from before the world was created.

Jesus became a big brother to the children Mary and Joseph conceived together. He had four brothers and several sisters. He grew up like any other little boy. His parents were attentive to His first tooth, His first step, His first word. They delighted in His little boy discovery of the world around Him. He was good with His little brothers and sisters. It was such fun to watch them together. He was so normal, in fact, that when He was twelve and stayed behind to talk with the religious leaders after the Feast asking questions and discussing spiritual things, His parents were frantic and asked Him why He would treat them like that. He had been missing and they had been searching for Him for three days! His reply is telling. "Did you not know I would be about my Father's business?" They did not know what He meant. So Jesus knew who His real Father was, but He submitted willingly to the care and parenting of Mary and Joseph until He was full grown and starting His public ministry at the age of thirty. He was in every way normal during all those years.

We know now that the growing-up years are formative of us as people. Jesus identifies with all of us. Typical family scenarios happened. His parents and siblings were not perfect. He was not rich and favored. He had the challenges of growing up around the neighbor kids. He had His share of hurts, misunderstandings, being falsely accused, and all the rest of normal life; but did not sin.

Discussion Questions

1. Read Luke 2. Imagine being with the shepherds that night. What do you feel? What do you see? What do you hear?

2. Imagine living next door to the boy Jesus. What was He like? Do you enjoy being friends and playmates? Why?

Chapter Twelve

Jesus, Unique Among Men

When Jesus turned thirty, He went to His cousin John to be baptized. John knew who He was and said, "I need to be baptized by you! Yet you come to me to be baptized?" Jesus said that this had to be done so all righteousness would be fulfilled. The people were coming to John to be baptized for repentance from sin, to turn from the unbelief that always grieves the Lord God. Jesus did not need to repent of anything but was sent to identify with each of us in our sin. He was not standoffish. He got right into our mess with us.

When He came up from being immersed under the river water, John saw the Holy Spirit of God fluttering down from Heaven and landing on Jesus and heard a voice, "This is my beloved Son in whom I am well pleased." Jesus' public ministry had begun. Father, Son and Holy Spirit were linked in declaring the kingdom of God was now here.

Remember that God made this world very good. The evil in it has been provided through the evil one. The Bible says the whole world lies in the lap of that enemy, but he is not the rightful owner of any of it. The kingdom of the Son was about to clash mightily with the counterfeit kingdom of darkness. Satan has no rightful claim to this world or its inhabitants. He lies, cheats and deceives to get people to believe his lies. People do believe the lies and are blinded to truth, but Jesus was about to begin reclaiming people to their rightful kingdom.

Jesus is the Way provided by our loving Creator-God for everyone who chooses to believe Him. He is the Truth. He is Life to everyone who believes. Everything He did was intentional obedience to the Father by the power of the Spirit to destroy the works of the evil one among the people. He deliberately confronted disease, death, demons, false teaching about the nature of God, and false assumptions about people. He displayed wonderful freedom from the culture wherever that culture defied God's viewpoint. He proclaimed the kingdom of God while walking among those caught in darkness. He invited all who would believe Him to follow Him in His kingdom of light, truth, and love.

He was radically different from all the other leaders of the political or religious worlds. He told Pilate that if His kingdom was of this world, i.e. a typical political kingdom, His servants would fight His arrest and crucifixion. But His kingdom was deeper, more foundational that any set up on the maps of the world. His kingdom is the intervention of the Creator-God into the darkness into which people are born. He invites all to believe the fundamental truth that God is and that He alone is good. We have no other way to return to the life-giving warmth of His love for us. We are corrupt. We cannot clean ourselves up, but now Jesus is come to declare freedom, healing, deliverance, sight, and hope through His willing sacrifice of Himself. He died for the sins of all who would ever believe.

People from every tribe and language group are destined for this kingdom. All over the world since the time of Jesus until now people have been hearing the claims of Jesus and believing Him. They have been changed. Their allegiance has been switched from selfishness to being centered on the Savior Jesus. God gives them new hearts. All who look to Him are radiant. Their faces are never covered with shame. Jesus truly made a way out of the dark. That kind of living comes so naturally to us. We are welcomed into our true nature. The original design is being restored as we believe Him daily. We are created in the image of God. We are destined to walk in good works which He prepares in advance for us to do. We are designed by Him. He is pleased with us, because we believe Jesus.

Millions throughout all the histories of the nations of the world have had their lives turned inside-out. Because Jesus took the penalty they deserved for siding with the enemy of their Creator, they are free to choose loyalty to the real King. They are now citizens of the real kingdom. They can live through the same Spirit that empowered Jesus lives of obedience to the same Father Jesus trusted and obeyed. They are free to be people like their Father and Savior: truthful, compassionate, loving, kind, just, joyful, peaceful, trusting, and hope filled. Throughout the ages and nations of the world the message has been confirmed by healing, deliverance from demons, signs and wonders by the power of God on display as His Word is taught and preached.

Jesus came to start the showdown between the evil one and God Almighty. He gave us the choice of which master to serve. He opened the way back to our loving Father-Creator. We are free to choose Him. Coming under His rule of us will make us very different people from what we are naturally. We become a kind of person who longs to become like Jesus. The Spirit empowers and transforms us as our minds change to agree with God about everything. We begin to really know our real Father, God.

Jesus was radical. He fits no model of this world. Let's watch as He confronts darkness in the lives of real people with real problems. See if your own heart is not drawn to Him like coming home out of a deep fog and long time away. Come and see Jesus.

Discussion Questions

1. How would you describe political leaders? Religious leaders?

2. Can you see how different Jesus is from them? Describe the differences.

3. Does Jesus' offer of restoration appeal to you? Why? What would be some consequences of deciding for Him and still living here?

Chapter Thirteen

Jesus and a Canaanite Woman

The Gospel of Matthew records an interesting story in chapter 15 in which not only a woman, but a non-Jewish woman, entreats Him for help. Let's read the narrative and then watch Jesus in this encounter.

> Jesus withdrew to the region of Tyre and Sidon. ²² A Canaanite woman from that vicinity came to him, crying out, "Lord, Son of David, have mercy on me! My daughter is suffering terribly from demon-possession."
>
> ²³ Jesus did not answer a word. So his disciples came to him and urged him, "Send her away, for she keeps crying out after us."
>
> ²⁴ He answered, "I was sent only to the lost sheep of Israel."
>
> ²⁵ The woman came and knelt before him. "Lord, help me!" she said.

[26] He replied, "It is not right to take the children's bread and toss it to their dogs."

[27] "Yes, Lord," she said, "but even the dogs eat the crumbs that fall from their masters' table."

[28] Then Jesus answered, "Woman, you have great faith! Your request is granted." And her daughter was healed from that very hour.

If Jesus truly came, as the Bible claims He did, to destroy the works of the evil one, there are a couple of issues here that need to be highlighted. First, the person beseeching Him for help is a woman. And, second, the person is not of Israel.

Women, like men, fell from their exquisite design of the image of God. They have, however, retained sensitivity to things being out of order as well as a deep desire for those they love to be whole. Sometimes women are seen as overly sensitive and told that they just need to accept things as they are and deal with it. But this woman was a mother of a girl who was tormented by what she knew to be demons. She must have heard about the numerous times Jesus was teaching about the kingdom of God and a person screamed out, "I know who You are, the holy One of God!!! Have You come to torment us before the time?" Jesus consistently told the demon to be quiet and come out of the person. And the demons obeyed. This was not a party trick. The true King was on the scene. His power and authority were real, no "magic words" or incantations are needed when you are genuinely in charge.

So the mother seeks Him out, acknowledging that He is descended from the great King of Israel, David. He says nothing to her to encourage her. His lack of interaction with her brings out of His followers the common response of the day much like today. 1. Jesus is an important person. 2. This person is annoying. 3. Jesus isn't responding. 4. Therefore, she being a foreigner and a woman must not merit His answer.

Jesus' statement about only being sent to the lost sheep of Israel seems cryptic and unkind, but her response indicates to me that He encouraged her on some level. It could also be that she had come to the desperate and genuine conclusion that if Jesus did not help, there was no help at all. What person or institution has authority to free from demonic harassment? In our day we like to ignore the subject, but when it is confirmed that this is the problem we cannot turn to the police, the government, the school officials, or the military. None of their authority extends to the supernatural realm. She fell on her knees before Jesus and acknowledged His authority, "Lord", and placed her concise plea before Him, "Help me!"

Then Jesus engages her in a way that brings out the truth of the cultural thinking, that those who are not Jews are dogs, and also allows her faith to be showcased. She must feel encouraged to engage in this conversation, even though it seems again to discourage any more appeals. "Even the dogs eat the crumbs that fall from their master's table."

There are not many cases recorded of Jesus being impressed with the faith of a person in need, but this is one of them. It does not matter that this is a woman, a foreigner. What matters is that her faith is placed squarely on Him. He is her only hope. She sees Him as capable of freeing her daughter when no one else on the planet can. She is not deterred by those who do not understand His authority or His heart. She presses in refusing to be dissuaded by any barriers until she has encountered Him for herself and heard from His mouth what He would say.

She is seen and heard and validated by Him. Her faith is well placed and her request is granted. From that hour her daughter is freed from the evil one. Can you imagine the mother arriving home and finding her daughter peaceful and in her right mind? Such a gift! Such a relief! Such a powerful deliverance! No showy words, He had not even seen the daughter. He healed her long distance with a word, which the faith-filled mother believed. Jesus cares for girls and women and foreigners. Jesus has power and greatness of spirit. Jesus is like no other person on the planet. And He is wonderful!

Discussion Questions

1. What circumstances are you in that have no one on earth to remedy?

2. What injury have you received that feels like will always haunt you, will always continue to bring evil fruit in your life?

3. What would it mean for you to take the desperate problem to Jesus? What would it mean to trust Him only to resolve the issue?

Chapter Fourteen

A Bleeding Woman's Testimony
(from Luke 8:43-38)

I am a woman of the nation of Israel. I was once strong and healthy, a mother, active, and not aware of what gifts all of that was. My husband was a fairly well-off businessman. We lived our lives together in a normal enough way. The children grew and married and moved away. My husband died. I became a widow, but had money from my husband, my loving children and my friends. Life was good enough.

Eventually my normal monthly cycles became less frequent. One came that went on for days, then weeks, then months, then years. For those not of Israel you must understand what this meant to my life. Not only was I scared of bleeding so long, but there are laws. I was considered unclean as long as I was issuing blood. I had to let people know so they would not touch me and become unclean themselves. I was isolated.

I took some of the money left me by my husband and went to see the doctor. He tried many things, some of them painful, before referring me to another doctor in another town. And so it went. It was now twelve long years. I had spent all the money and seen all the doctors. I was weak, sickly. I didn't know what to do.

One of my neighbors told me one day of a new teacher in Israel named Jesus. The stories about Him were wonderful. He had healed blind people, lame people, lepers, and even raised a dead boy at the funeral! I got to thinking about Him. Surely this man of God who could do such things could help me.

Later my town was buzzing with excitement one morning, Jesus was passing through! I could not let this opportunity pass. I would not disturb Him. I would not want to make Him unclean, but I was desperate! There were so many people! Then I thought, "If I could just touch the hem of His garment, I would be healed." Surely that would not be too much to ask. I would not have to bother anyone.

So I left the house and followed the noise of the crowd. I saw the direction they were headed and went along a side street to get a little ahead of them. Then I cut over to the street the crowd was on. I saw Him then. It had to be Him. Everyone was asking Him questions and looking at Him. I pressed my way through the crowd until I was close behind Him and reached ahead and down until I could just touch . . . the hem of His garment. There!

Immediately warmth passed through me and I knew I was healed! It worked! I was not bleeding anymore and I was strong and well again! Oh, bless God for sending such a teacher as this to our little town!

But then, the procession stopped. Everyone came to a standstill. The Teacher was looking around. He said something to His disciples.

They answered Him, but He still stood looking around at the crowd near Him. Finally, His words made their way to my ears as the crowd repeated what He had said to His men. "Somebody has touched Me. Power has gone out from me." The disciples did not know what He meant since the press of the crowd was so great, but I knew.

After several minutes, I knew I must speak up. He was not just going to move on. So, I pressed through the narrow wall of people between Him and me. He saw me. I told Him all I had gone through the past twelve years and of my plan to simply touch the hem of His garment.

I was not sure of what His reaction would be. The teachers of our day were not ones who liked to be interrupted or touched, certainly not by anyone unclean. They were holy men, separate from the rest of us. I was nervous, but then, I had been made whole, hadn't I? I had had to tell Him.

As I looked up to see what He would say, my eyes met His. I have never seen such understanding in the eyes of anyone. It was like He really saw what I had suffered all these years socially, financially, physically. Beyond that, though, He saw me. He knew me and with His look validated me as a person. I was not just a worthless woman to this man. I was a daughter in Israel, precious to Israel's God. I thought of how Hagar must have felt when she named the Lord "the One who sees me."

He spoke then as the crowd became deathly quiet. "Woman, your faith has healed you. Go in peace."

He was not angry with me! He did not make a public display of the worthlessness of women. He affirmed that my faith had been rightly placed, squarely on Him. He had blessed me with wholeness, wellness, and peace. He had been my only hope, and He welcomed me to hope in Him.

I went home in great joy with energy to spare and told everyone who would listen what a miracle He did that day! All the doctors I could find could not bring relief. He, by my simply touching His garment, healed me completely. Bless the Lord God!

Discussion Questions

1. Have you exhausted other resources looking for a solution? Maybe doctors, psychologists, social workers, judges, and other professionals have hit a wall. They cannot help you.

2. Can you consider that Jesus is the expert? Can you consider that He alone has all power and authority? Can you press through whatever obstacles are in your way to reach through to trust Him? Will you?

Chapter Fifteen

An Adulterous Woman
(John 8:1-11)

The two women we have encountered so far with Jesus had needs. One's daughter was tormented by a demon. The other woman through no fault of her own had a bleeding problem. Jesus helped the first by granting her request in response to her great faith, not even seeing the daughter. He helped the second before He even saw her coming, and then affirmed that her faith had made her whole. But what would He do with a woman who was guilty? Does she get a different response from Him than from her religious neighbors and other leaders of the religious establishment of the time? Let us see.

I do not know how you, dear reader, feel about the dawn; but I have loved the growing light, the freshness of the morning air, and the awakening of the world as the sun makes its appearance. I have watched sunrises almost everywhere I have been: Oceanside, camping in the woods, and now in the mountains. Every morning is fresh, even cloudy or rainy ones. There is expectancy in that time of day. It is a new day waiting to be walked into, a fresh page waiting for the story to be written on it.

On this particular day Jesus was in the temple courts at dawn. The air was fresh. The day was new. The heat had not yet risen on the land. A crowd surrounded Him already, expectant, eager to hear what this teacher had to say. What a wonderful opportunity to listen to one who claimed to be directly from the Lord God Himself! The signs and wonders confirmed everything He said. His message and His ministry went together. Wisdom and power met in this one man more clearly than in anyone in all the history of the world. He had wisdom greater than Solomon, their beloved third king and displayed power greater than that displayed by even Moses. And He was here in Jerusalem ready to speak to whoever came to the open areas around the temple. He spoke of God and His kingdom, and the people were more than ready to hear.

That was the main problem. What He said was not just rehashed opinions of ancient writers. He was not guessing at truth and making harsh rules and demands of the people. He did not speak to them as though the Almighty who sees everything wanted to squash them. It has been noted that one goal of religion is to keep the people under control. We are only too familiar with religious cultures where certain things are done and certain things are not. It pretty much ends up like a glorified children's club. "We're in. You're out." This arrangement gives its leaders great power over the people. Fear is the motivation behind what the people do or do not do in order to be "acceptable."

Here comes Jesus with a message of invitation to step out of the influence of man-made, man-controlled, fear-based cultural living. He opened their minds to a way back into relationship with the God who created everything. This was the God who loved His creation, the God who alone remained good when all else fell into darkness. He told them they could follow Him, the Light, and not walk in darkness anymore. He provided a real "alternate lifestyle."

He talked with, ate with, and engaged in the lives of people on the "outs" with the religious "in crowd." The people loved Him for it. He was a breath of fresh air. But the power mongers of the religious system did not like it one bit. He dared to challenge their way of doing things, dared to show them their fault in neglecting mercy, kindness, and compassion as they fulfilled the tiny details of the law.

He had to be stopped, according to them. You see in the gospel accounts many times that these leaders conspired together to make Him fall. They even were in cahoots with Herod's gang of enforcers. They sent lawyers. They set up "law breaking" traps with sick people. They wanted their control back. They wanted Him dead.

So, that early morning as Jesus sat down to teach the people, a group of these leaders burst into the courts with a woman in tow. They had caught this woman in the very act of adultery. What did the teacher have to say to that? Moses said that such a person was to be stoned. What did the Teacher say?

They thought they had Him. If He said the woman should be stoned, He would be going against the Romans who alone had the right of execution in the lands they occupied. The peoples they had conquered were not allowed to put people to death. They had to bring them to Roman courts. And if Jesus said she should go free, then He could be accused of breaking the Law of Moses. Therefore, He could not possibly be from God as He clearly claimed to be.

Let us take a moment to look at the law God gave them through Moses. It did have a lot to say about sexually deviant behavior. People were only to have sexual intimacy with their marital partners after they were married. It was to be a marriage between a man and a woman. There was to be no incest, no bestiality, no same-sex encounters, no extra-marital union. Leviticus 20:10 states, "If a man commits adultery with another man's wife—with the wife of his neighbor—both the adulterer and the adulteress must be put to death."

So, the leaders caught the woman in the act of adultery by herself? Where was the man? How exactly do you catch someone doing this? Sounds to me like a set-up. How do you find a man who is willing to take a married woman and bed her knowing they will be caught? And he gets off free because he helped her get caught? What exactly was the arrangement here?

The leaders who set this up . . . how desperate were they for them to get involved in this decidedly unholy activity? They, perhaps, waited outside the bedroom window, outside the door? Did they pay the man off? How did they know of this ripe affair? What else did they know about the sins of the people? Did they care at all what God Himself thought about anything?

Jesus is sitting while teaching the people. The leaders have forced the woman into the center of the crowd and made her to stand in front of all the people. I see her standing near Jesus, shaking and fearful. The

Jews were passionate people. This could easily become the last morning of her life.

She had been looking for someone who would love her. That's how she came to be in another man's bed besides her husband's. She was looking for someone to cherish her, care for her, see her as valuable. Then these religious men come bursting in and drag her off. He was not taken. He had betrayed her? Given her over to the authorities? Exposed her sinful behavior without taking any responsibility himself? She was exposed with no help in sight.

I don't know whether she had heard of Jesus yet. If she had, she must have heard He was a holy man. If He was like the "holy men" of her day, she could not expect anything but condemnation from Him. If she had not heard about Him, she at least could tell that He was to be her judge. There was no one to speak for her, no one to tell of the heartache that had driven her to seek shelter in a forbidden place, no one who would speak of the betrayal yet again of her trust.

Jesus does not play their game. He bends down and begins to write in the dust. The teachers of the law and the Pharisees, who had designed this perfect plan, had brought her there and forced her to stand in front of everyone. In their hopes to trap Him they must have been angrily confused. "What's He doing?!? Why doesn't He answer us? Our plan was perfectly set up, perfectly executed. What is the hold up?" Please notice that these men were not bothered by using people to get what they wanted. Happens all the time, doesn't it? We may even have done that a time or two ourselves, right? I guarantee it was not lost on Jesus either.

After a while He stood and said, "He that is without sin, let him cast the first stone." Then He stooped down and wrote in the dust again.

Well, that was quite a shift of focus! First, it was the woman's evident evil behavior, no matter what the motivation. Now, it is each of our evil behavior, thoughts, and speech on trial. Who would be qualified to cast that first stone?

The older ones left first. Honestly, with more years comes more revelation of our own falseness, our own participation in what is clearly not good. We don't become better and better with age automatically. We do have the opportunity to face ourselves and think.

As the younger ones see the older ones leaving, they think of sins they have done. They all walk away, even the crowd who had come to hear Jesus at first as the day dawned. Only the woman and Jesus are left. She was amazed, I am sure, at the diffusing of a violent confrontation, but still unsure of what He would say.

Some day each of us will stand alone before the Judge of the whole world. No one else's opinion of us will matter. All those who supported us, all who condemned and hated us will be mute. What will He say?

Jesus was still stooped down. He straightened then and stood, faced her and asked, "Woman, where are they? Has no one accused you?" As her eyes met His and she saw no angry condemnation there, she answered, "No one, sir."

Could that be right? Within the last hour she had been in bed with a man she thought loved her, burst in upon by powerful religious leaders, dragged to the temple courts that were brimming with people, and made to stand in front of this man of God. No one was left to accuse, condemn, or cast the first stone? That one would be followed by hundreds of other stones until she was dead. There was no first stone cast? No one left to throw it?

"Then neither do I condemn you. Go now and leave your life of sin."

In that moment profound understanding washed over her. God didn't want her dead. God wanted her to live the noble life He intended for His created ones to live. He wanted her to take refuge in His love for her, His fathomless understanding of her, and His willingness to let all her past go so she could walk into newness for the rest of her days.

Never again would she seek a mere man for her ultimate comfort, provision, protection, or safety. She had faced God Himself and found mercy where she deserved none. She had received grace. She would never be the same again. No more sinning. She had now seen the face of God, loving and kind. She would stay connected to Him no matter the cost because He had become her sure and certain hope.

Discussion Questions

1. Have you ever done, or thought of doing, something very wrong? Something you would not want anyone to know? Can you identify with this woman caught in adultery? Can you feel her guilt and shame?

2. Is Jesus soft on sin? Does He say by His actions in this story that it is OK to do what is against the Law of God?

3. Can you see how the heart is the focus of Jesus? The hearts of the conspirators, as well as the assembled crowd, were revealed. The woman's heart was won over by His deliverance of her. Jesus is all about what is going on in our hearts. Will you trust yours to Him?

Chapter Sixteen

A Social Outcast
(John 4)

In this chapter I would like to introduce you to a woman who is part of a group rejected by the Jews and by her own people. Such a woman is a mixture of need and hardening. She has to harden herself to the realities of other people's rejection of her. She is resigned to being invisible, unloved, uninvited to community events, not sought out for friendship. Her world is one devoid of positive human interaction. She has been shunned by Jews because of her birth into the wrong descendants of ancient Israel. She has been shunned by her own people due to her number of marital and bed partners.

We find Jesus and His disciples having to leave Judea. The religious leaders had found out through their spies that Jesus was now baptizing more disciples than John the Baptist. Jesus wasn't actually the one doing the immersing. His disciples did that, but the fact remained that He was a growing threat to the leaders by His increasing popularity. John had been the first real threat to their religious monopoly, but

Herod took off his head. Now this Jesus whom John announced was capturing more hearts and minds than John did.

So Jesus and His disciples were headed back to Galilee. Most Jews would travel well out of their way to avoid going through the lands of the Samaritans, the "contaminated" line of the Hebrews. But Jesus "had" to go through Samaria by His Father's instruction. About noon Jesus was tired and sat to rest by a well near the town of Sychar. For those of you who know the original family tree of Israel, this well was dug by Jacob (Israel) and given to his son, Joseph (the one who became second to Pharaoh in the time of a great famine), as an inheritance. Water sources are a precious thing in arid lands. The disciples went into town to try to find food.

Jesus is alone by the well when our woman approaches to get her daily household water. Most women get their water early in the day, near dawn; but ours finds the interaction with the other women more painful than companionable. So, she comes in the heat of the day when no one will make her feel like she does not belong with "decent" women.

Jesus begins to make His way past all the defenses and into her place of need. He will not be dissuaded until she sees hope for herself in God.

He asks her for a drink. That is rather stunning to her. "How is it that you, being a Jew, ask me for a drink?" Evidently, Jews severely limited their interactions with Samaritans, not even talking to them if that could be avoided.

Jesus is not put off by her reference to prejudice. "If you knew the gift of God and who it is who asks you for a drink, you would have asked Him and He would have given you living water." Jesus is not just playing mind games with her here. Truly, the gift of God is forgive-ness, cleansing, and newness of life. God has always provided a way back to relationship with Him. He was about to make The Way clear. Living water is intriguing to her, but so is another fact.

"Sir, the well is deep and you have nothing to draw with. Where will you get this living water? Are you greater than our father Jacob who gave us this well and drank from it himself and his sons and his flocks and herds?" She knows some of the common history with the "pure" Jews. The patriarchs were highly esteemed by both Jews and Samaritans. She seems a bit sarcastic here. Perhaps she has been disappointed by the empty comments of men before.

"Everyone who drinks this water will be thirsty again, but whoever drinks the water I give him will never thirst. Indeed, the water I give him will become in him a spring of water welling up to eternal life."

She hears the part about not thirsting again and goes for it. "Sir, give me this water so I won't get thirsty and have to keep coming back here to draw water." How labor saving, having a source of water so handy!

Jesus shifts away from the daily need for water to a more personal subject. "Go, call your husband and come back." Perhaps this is a "heads up" that we are about to go into deeper water and He wants her husband in on the coming discussion.

She balks. "I have no husband." Jesus fills in the blanks with truth about her having had five husbands and the man she now has is not her husband. Wow! He commends her on saying that she has no husband.

Imagine her amazement that He knows so much about her, and yet does not seem upset with her, nor is He judging her. He is keeping the conversation peaceful and moving toward truth.

She changes the subject and talks about some religious differences between Samaritans and Jews about the place to worship. She senses that He is a prophet, so here is a concern worth addressing, in her mind at least. He goes deeper, "Believe me, woman, a time is coming when you will worship the Father neither on this mountain nor in Jerusalem. You Samaritans worship what you do not know; we worship what we do know, for salvation is from the Jews. Yet a time is coming and has now come when the true worshipers will worship the Father in spirit and truth, for they are the kind of worshipers the Father seeks. God is spirit, and his worshipers must worship in spirit and in truth."

Jesus is not talking about merely behavior, routines, or ceremonies. He is getting to the very nature of God Himself. He is Spirit. He is Father. He is good. He made people with the ability to join their spirits to His in truthful, joyful, warm, loving, safe, victorious worship of Him. Jesus was here to restore that ability for all who would believe Him. This is a powerful revelation. Jesus makes it to one foreign, despised woman. We would probably counsel Him to have shared that gem with a large audience, or at least a more important person. She is nobody to anybody, except to God.

She pulls up the shadow of a hope Jews had held onto for centuries. "I know that Messiah is coming. When He comes, He will explain everything to us."

"I who speak to you am He," Jesus declared.

This is one of the most candid revelations of Jesus about Himself that He ever makes. And He makes it to her! A nobody! But can you see a glimpse into the heart of God? It is essential to God the Father that this particular woman come to hope in His Son. He sends Jesus into a territory that most Jews avoid. He sends her to His Son at the well at noon on her regular routine, which God fully knows. And He tells Jesus to reveal to this alienated woman His heart's desire for genuine worship from the spirit of people and in truth. No more of these fake gestures! God wanted people who would love Him from their hearts. It would not matter then where they worshipped from. The Father tells Jesus to reveal to her that He is the Messiah everyone has been waiting for.

Just then the disciples return. You know how you have walked into a situation where a deep conversation is going on? There is this sense of, "Am I interrupting something?" Just so it is here. Their beloved Teacher is not only in the vicinity of a woman, but is actually talking to her! What He just said was of major consequence in her life by her reaction to it. They wanted to ask Him why He was talking to her or to ask her what she wanted; but they did not dare. Something was clearly going on here that was beyond them.

She leaves her water pot there at the well and runs into the town. This woman was alight with a fire no one would have believed possible. Instead of quietly going about her usual business avoiding eye contact or drawing attention to herself, she is telling everyone she sees, "Come, see a man who told me everything I ever did! Could this be the Christ?" There is no shame in her anymore about her past. He knew all about it, and He still offered her incredible truth! God loved her and wanted the worship from her own spirit. Truth is acceptable to God! No more hiding!

Because of her the townspeople come out to Jesus and invite Him to stay with them. Many believed in Him because of the woman's words about Him (and the readily apparent change in her), but after hearing Jesus for themselves over the course of two days, many believed Him on their own. They said they really knew this man is the Savior of the world! No more walls between the woman and the town. No more of that game. They were all in awe together of the One who was and is the Promised One from God! It was a new town after that visit. Jesus had gone off the beaten track and His presence had transformed a woman's life and that of her whole village. No one is too small, or too unimportant for God's notice.

The disciples, by the way, get another insight into the kingdom of God. They had gone into the town to find food, right? So, they encourage Jesus to eat after the woman left. He said He had food to eat that they knew nothing about. They wondered if someone had given Him something, but He said that doing what the Father told Him to do was deeply satisfying. That was real food. Watching the woman believe Him, seeing her change into a woman with great hope in God was worth the hot travel and the weary waiting by the well.

He then drew a verbal picture for them. They could also be part of this satisfying work. They could participate in a harvest of eternal souls. They could lift their eyes and look. They would be enabled to see others who were "ripe" for believing, others the world looked through, but that God saw and desired to be brought to Him. They could be part of the greatest rescue mission ever in history—God reaching to people through His Son and seeing them saved by believing Him.

An alien woman becomes a daughter of the King, and she brings a whole town to the Messiah, even in "contaminated" Samaria.

Discussion Questions

1. Have you ever felt that you were an outcast, not quite good enough? Have you ever treated someone else like that?

2. Has a conversation ever changed your life? Do you think a conversation with Jesus would? Will you believe Him, too?

Chapter Seventeen

The Woman with the Ointment
(Matt. 26:6-13, Mark 14:3-9, Luke 7:36-50, John 12:1-8)

Reading the Gospels we see Jesus ministering, healing, teaching, casting out demons; but this story is unique because in it one woman ministers to Jesus. All four Gospels tell this story. As with any traffic accident, there are variations due to the different vantage points of the eye witnesses; but I believe all four accounts are of the same event. I will blend them together for you, so you may get a full picture of what is happening here.

The story takes place in Bethany in the home of a Pharisee, Simon. It is six days before the Passover when Jesus will be crucified. Lazarus, whom Jesus raised from the dead, was there. His sister Martha is among the servers.

Diane Sillaman

There is much tension in the air. The Pharisees, Sadducees and teachers of the law were looking for a way to arrest Jesus and have Him put to death. This desire started in them a while back, but had escalated with the resurrection of Lazarus. Many Jews had been to his funeral and the mourning time after his death. Jesus had come after Lazarus had been in the grave four days already. After praying, Jesus told the people to remove the stone from the mouth of the grave. Then, He commanded Lazarus to come out. And he did!!! Jesus then had them unwrap the grave clothes and let him go. They did, and Lazarus was fully alive once again, completely well. The Jews that were there rejoiced, amazed. Can you imagine the desire to hear Lazarus' story? How often did he tell what Jesus had done?

Some of those who saw the resurrection went and told the religious leaders. They did not rejoice. They were fretful that the whole world would go after Jesus. He raised the dead man, who had been dead for days!!! What could they possibly do now?!?

Notice that there seems to be no thought that God could actually be among them. Wouldn't you think that those who made their living in one way or another handling God's things would be overjoyed to welcome the One who showed by teaching and miracles that He was God's Son? Shouldn't they be first in line to welcome Him? But in John 11:48 they say in their war counsel, "If we let him go on thus, every one will believe in him, and the Romans will come and destroy both our holy place and our nation." They had set up their place of power and position, awe and authority by using God's things. They were not interested in the reality of God. They had made a cozy nest for themselves in God's stuff. They did not care about the real God giving real hope to the people He loved. Their rules made life burdensome to the people. Jesus had called them on that many times. No, the enmity they had for Him was palpable, strong, and deadly.

Mary, the younger of Lazarus' sisters, enters the dining room where the men are reclined on cushions their heads toward the table enjoying the supper. She has with her an alabaster jar of exquisitely expensive nard ointment. She pours it on Jesus' head and feet. Weeping, she sheds tears on His feet and wipes them with her hair. She is broken over her sin, adoring of Him for His mercy, and expressing to Him her love and her knowledge that He is being plotted against. She senses the deadly hostility between the religious establishment and Jesus. Jesus said she did this to prepare Him to be buried. She saw the handwriting on the wall, so to speak. His days were short.

This was unusual behavior to be sure. You would think that the men dining with Jesus might be touched at her elaborate display of heart-felt love. But there were two reactions, neither of them kind.

Simon, the host, said to himself, "If this man were a prophet, he would have known who and what sort of woman this is who is touching him, for she is a sinner." Well, there you have it. He doubts Jesus' identity. He disapproves of her physical contact with Him, even though it is non-sexual. He rejects her, sees her as without any value, due to her well known sinful lifestyle.

Judas, one of Jesus' own disciples, stirred up the other disciples making them indignant over the waste of this valuable perfume. Why, it could be sold for a lot of money and the money given to the poor! Judas was the treasurer for the group, also a thief. He would often take for himself what was given to Jesus for ministry. He had no interest in helping the poor. He saw this scene as a now wasted possibility of having a whole lot more money to help himself to.

These violently negative reactions were not lost on Jesus. What would He say? How did He feel about what she had done? Would He also mock and condemn her? Would He treat her as a mindless woman, unworthy of credit? Will He bend to public pressure?

To Simon He tells a story about two debtors. One owed a whole lot of money to a guy. The other owed a little bit. The lender in compassion for them when they could not pay forgave them both all their debt. Then, He asked, "Now which of them will love him more?" Simon guesses, "The one, I suppose, to whom he forgave more."

"That's right," Jesus said. Then He gives him a lesson in hospitality. "I entered your house, you gave me no water for my feet, but she has wet my feet with her tears and wiped them with her hair. You gave me no kiss, but from the time I came in she has not ceased to kiss my feet. You did not anoint my head with oil, but she has anointed my feet with ointment. Therefore I tell you, her sins, which are many, are forgiven, for she loved much; but he who is forgiven little, loves little."

The hospitality of the Middle East is thorough and generous. These oversights of Simon were pointed. He was in effect saying that he would invite Jesus to dinner and then put Him in His place. He was actively insulting Jesus by omitting the most basic cultural routines: washing feet, a welcoming kiss on one or both cheeks, and oil for the head. Jesus could have made a scene as these expected treatments were withheld, but He did not. He does not play games with us. Insults are noted, but do not deter Him from listening to the Father and doing what He says to do.

Simon and his buddies liked to think of themselves as good. They did many things to prove their innocence and righteousness. They kept away from persons of lesser moral character lest they become contaminated. They lived in the illusion that they did not need to be forgiven. They had no sin. Really?!? How about plotting the death of the only truly innocent man in the world, whom you invited to dinner?

We are not so very different, though, are we? We try very hard to justify or rationalize everything we do, positioning ourselves in our minds so that we have no guilt. We feel we do not need to be forgiven. We are saying in effect that Jesus' sacrifice for us on the cross was unnecessary. We do not want to look at how far from being like Jesus, the standard of perfection, we actually are. In truth all of us have much to be forgiven for every day.

Jesus says the one who is forgiven much loves much. He says to the woman, Mary, "Your sins are forgiven. Your faith has saved you; go in peace." There is uproar at His taking God's place in forgiving sins. "Who is this, who even forgives sins?" Jesus could not do anything right in their eyes, could He? But He did not let their judgments stop Him from giving her a new lease on life. The past is cleansed now. Her faith in Him is well placed. It will allow her to now live in peace, purity, and loving unity with Almighty God. She saw Him for who He was and risked being scorned by men to express her gratitude for His mercy towards her. Jesus rewards her honesty about her evil behavior and her belief that He could remove what stood between her and a holy God. Her gratitude spills over into floods of love for Jesus Himself. And He loves her. Their circle of light and love is not diminished by the lack of understanding of them by the others in the room.

To the disciples, who are so concerned about the economic waste, He says, "Why do you trouble the woman? She has done a beautiful thing to me. For you always have the poor with you, and whenever you will, you can do good to them; but you will not always have me. She has done what she could; she has anointed my body beforehand for burying. Truly, I say to you, wherever this gospel is preached in the whole world, what she has done will be told in memory of her."

Talk about redirection in a few words! He sees that their words are troubling to her. Maybe she thought, "Oh no! Perhaps He would rather have had me care for the poor with this nard." He tells them to stop bothering her. He protects her from His own disciples!

Secondly, He takes what she has done as a personal gift to Him. Who else ever did such a beautiful thing to Him? He spent His life doing many beautiful things for others, but this act is unique in Jesus' eyes. He appreciates her care for Him.

Thirdly, although concern for the poor sounds good, no one has to wait to have a year's wages before sharing with the poor. He can give what he has. Were they giving out of compassion for the poor now? There are always poor people handy. They would appreciate any help.

Fourthly, they would not always have Him. I wonder if at this point the disciples thought about the many times He told them that He would be betrayed and handed over to the authorities and put to death. He told them, but maybe it was so unthinkable they couldn't take it in. She understood, though, and was actually preparing His precious body for the grave. The fragrance of the nard filled the whole house. I wonder if some of the beauty of that gift still lingered on His skin while He hung on the cross.

And lastly, He sets up a verbal, ongoing memorial to her. In all the nations where the gospel would be carried down through the centuries until the end of the world, what she had done would be told in memory of her. She was not just a worthless, sin-laden woman. She had seen in Jesus the hope of cleansing and a new beginning. If she lost all else, she would cling to her love of Him. She saw Him as God come in the flesh. He was her only hope.

The same enemies that sought to keep her down were the ones who passionately wanted Jesus taken out. They were also plotting the possibility of removing Lazarus. Many people believed in Jesus because of His bringing Lazarus back from the dead. He was actually eating at the table when all this drama was going on.

Jesus exalts this woman forever. He couples His story with hers; He the Savior of the whole world, she the one who saw and believed Him.

Discussion Questions

1. How do you think she knew Jesus' enemies were getting ready to kill him?

2. Do you think she felt the hostility from the religious leaders towards herself? Did they offer hope for her to be different from her past?

3. Like Judas do we sometimes have ulterior motives for "good deeds"? Was Mary trying to "look good" or was she deeply driven to show her care and gratitude? Discuss motivations.

4. What would it mean to you, if you were in Jesus' place, to have one person truly get how amazingly unique you were? . . . For one person to understand the incredible pressure from their concerted opposition to Him? For one person to see that your death was coming quickly?

Chapter Eighteen

Women and Jesus

The apostle John wrote, "Jesus did many other things as well. If every one of them were written down, I suppose that even the whole world would not have room for the books that would be written." I would like for us to look at other places in the Gospel accounts where Jesus and women were in the same time and place.

Jesus taught people all the time. There often were women in the crowd. We are told of at least two times where He took a small amount of food (a few fish and a few loaves of bread) and fed those He was teaching. Once was a group of 5,000+, another time a group of 4,000+. In both those groups were women and children. He cared for people. He knew they had come from distant parts and would need nourishment before going home. He did not seem to mind that women and children learned from Him as well as men. He had come for all.

After one of those times, the people pursued Him the following day because they wanted more food. Jesus told them they were to eat the Bread from Heaven, Him. Their fathers had eaten manna everyday in the wilderness for decades. But now He said He was the true Bread from Heaven, that His flesh was real food and His blood real drink. All men, women, and children were to rely on Him for new life. He was giving everything He was in order for us to be genuinely connected to God again. The connection was lost when Adam and Eve believed Satan. It would be restored by believing Jesus.

Women were in probably in the group that Jesus was teaching when He said that His words were spirit and they were life. Believing what Jesus said was the key to entering this new kingdom of God. Men, women and children were being invited to believe what He said.

Another time He told crowds that anyone wanting to come after Him must take up his/her cross (an agent of death) every day, deny him/herself, and follow Him. This was a hard saying. The Romans crucified the most shameful, guilty offenders. But the new life in Him requires that we die to our old one, the one in which we decide what we want and how to get it. The old life is centered on self. The new one has God's way as its center. Men, women and children were being called to give up what they thought was living and follow Him into a life dedicated to knowing and living for God. This was very new teaching. Jesus brought God close. He was calling all to a new life.

Jesus told parables in which He was the Bridegroom. I believe the women hearing these references were overjoyed. They knew that a Bridegroom takes care of everything concerning the bride. A good husband, which He certainly would be, would give her His name, would provide for her, cherish her as His own dear wife, and protect and defend her. He would leave her, but only for a while and only to prepare a place for her to live with Him at His Father's house. The bride would be expecting

Him to return for her when the time was right. This common custom of the time was a perfect illustration of what was truly happening between Jesus and His people. All the emotions of hope, wonder, anticipation, and longing are rightly placed on Jesus and our future with Him.

The perspective on their lives changed because of being in relationship with Jesus. He had entered their lives, taught them truth, healed, delivered, and won their hearts. The women who believed Him would never be the same. Now they had Someone bigger, richer, more powerful than anyone else in the Universe, who loves, sees and understands them. God Himself had entered their lives. These women found rest in the middle of life's demands because they had been made alive in Jesus. They could live the lives He would soon die for them to have: lives of joy, hope, peace, promise, purpose, and above all, love. They, the feminine image of God, would once again be connected to their Creator, who loved them still. What hope! What value they still had, no matter what kind of darkness they had been involved in! They intuitively knew Jesus was sent by God as no other had been, that He was exactly like God . . . far more wonderful than they had dreamed. He was not hard, cold, angry, and remote. He was warm, real, truthful, and here with them . . . no condemnation.

In Jesus women find an unending source of pure love. They now would be able to drink in all they desire at any moment. Being in love puts wings on a woman's spirit. She was designed by her Creator to be fulfilled to the degree that she is loved. It was God's love at the beginning that made woman OK, more than OK. Now forgiveness of sin was available. The Way back into personal friendship with God is opened by believing the Son of God. She can be confident that He is guiding her every step, providing for her every need, and loving her the whole time. She is safe because her Bridegroom adores her and is with her always.

I believe the women who followed Jesus caring for His needs knew what I am talking about. At the crucifixion when all the disciples fled (except John), a group of women stayed. They even followed to see what happened to His body. Why would they risk the possibility that the Romans would slay them, too? I believe that they had tasted the love they were created for in Jesus. They could not leave the horrible scene. The One their hearts lived for was betrayed, beaten, and killed. Still they would not leave. I think they figured they were as good as dead without Him anyway. He was their life. He had become their reason to live. They knew the awful facts of the events that day. They were there. They could not be anywhere else while the love of their lives, the hope of their hearts was put to death.

Three days later the women did not expect Him to rise anymore than the disciples did. They were bringing spices to anoint His body. Only the body was not in the grave. Angelic messengers told them He was alive! Jesus appeared first to women. Reconnecting with them was close to His and His Father's heart. Their hope had been rightly placed in Him. He was alive forever now that they penalty of sin was paid in full. When the women told the disciples that they had seen Him alive, they thought the women were crazy. But the women knew Him. They had seen Him. They believed Him.

Since Jesus left earth, He has continued to call to men, women and children. Here are some of the things that happened after He returned to the Father.

After Jesus ascended, He told His disciples to wait in Jerusalem for His promise. There were 120 people in an upper room the day the promise was fulfilled. Women were in the group when the Holy Spirit came for the first time to indwell those who believed Jesus. They spoke in tongues as well. Peter, while explaining these wonderful things, quoted from the prophet Joel. "In the last days, God says, I will pour out my Spirit on all people. Your sons and daughters will prophesy, your young men will see visions, your old men will dream dreams. Even on my servants, both men and women, I will pour out my Spirit in those days, and they will prophesy."

Women were instrumental in the building of the early church. They were right beside the men in prayer, fellowship and worship. Paul personally thanked some of them in his letters for their valiant work for the Gospel alongside of him.

Women are no more and no less capable of being vessels filled with the treasure of Jesus. Jesus welcomed people, healed them, delivered them, taught them, and invited them into His kingdom whether male or female. All people need to be restored to the Creator. Jesus is the Way back to the Father's loving heart. The power of God is released to make sons and daughters of God out of rebellious, lost people. Jesus gives this power to whoever receives Him. Adoption into God's family is open to those who believe.

God created male and female in His image. He fulfilled Adam and Eve's hearts before the Fall. Jesus came to restore the image. As men and women believe Him, they are gradually changed more and more into the likeness of their Lord. They become more and more like their design: peaceful, loving, joyful, humble, gentle, and fulfilled.

Jesus showed the love and power of God. He paid the debt of death we all owe for our sin. He rose again, ascended back to the Father to make a place for us who believe, and sent His Spirit on men and women who believe Him. He is the Hope of the hopeless, the Help of the helpless, and the Rescuer of all who will turn from darkness to believe in Him who is the Light. Women and men alike are invited to repent and believe the Great News that Jesus opened the Way back to loving relationship with the Father, our Creator. Jesus is unique for all time in the whole Universe. He is finding His sheep and bringing them home.

Discussion Questions

1. The women who were in the crowds that were fed those days, what would that have been like? Use your imagination. How would you feel that He cared to feed your family? Women usually see to the feeding of their families. Maybe they didn't realize they would stay that long. Can you sense their relief and gratitude for the thorough feeding of their families?

2. The women who stayed, who cried over Jesus at His death, why do you think they stayed? Why would you?

3. What do you think the women felt the morning of the resurrection who heard the angels? Who saw Jesus alive? Who told the disciples the news?

Chapter Nineteen

Woman's Role in Winning the World

The world marred by sin is quickly coming to an appointed end. The time is closer now than it has ever been. Scripture gives signs of the end. Many of them are clear in our world today. There are still many people who are going to respond to the message of Jesus Christ. Many others will come to believe on Jesus, the One God sent into this world to live, die, and rise again from the dead. How do women fit in this winning of hearts to Jesus, this great harvest at the world's end?

First, God has placed each woman in a unique circle of influence. No two women know exactly the same people. Even where spheres of influence overlap, no two women have the same relationship with the third party. You have experienced this. Think of the women in your life. Are any two identical in their impact on you? No. Each one has her own "flavor" in your life. When a woman drops out of your life for whatever reason, does anyone truly take her place? No. Each is irreplaceable. Even the ones who cause us great pain are unique. Women are influential in the lives of people by God's design.

Second, women who follow Jesus are different kind of women. They have troubles, which they bring to Him for His control. They suffer insults, scorn, mocking, and abuse; but they turn to the One who suffered vicious, undeserved cruelty out of His love for them. They receive from Him the grace to forgive the offenders, to love and pray for them. These precious women find no one on the face of the earth who loves them like God Himself does. They are content to draw from Him the love and security their spirits crave.

Third, these women interact differently with people. Their contented, well loved spirits make an influence of grace wherever they go. They are not bound by social conventions. They are free to be kind and care for those who are not "socially acceptable" just like Jesus did. They do not have to defend themselves with harsh words. They are free to remain quiet and gentle in the face of hostility just like Jesus was. They are not afraid. They know that Almighty God is their defender and protector. They have confidence that no suffering on their part is wasted. They trust God. They simply, generously care for people who are used to being overlooked. They have nothing to prove, no scale to be measured by, no rules to keep. The Judge of all the earth has seen their faith and given them pardon. He guides them through their daily lives. Gradually they grow away from the dark and into the Light.

Fourth, the "kindness of God," which leads to lives being turned around, flows out in loving waves from His daughters. Everyone in their spheres of influence is affected by women who know and love Jesus, women whom Jesus knows and loves. The children in their households have the gift of loving moms who look to God for wisdom in raising them. The husbands have to admit that their wives' deep faith is a stabilizing blessing to them. Neighbors, clerks in stores, fast food people and servers in restaurants are blessed by the "other's focus" of these daughters of the King. They are not demanding, complaining, and whiny women. They are helpful, patient, peaceful, and wise.

Fifth, the truth of the gospel falls gently from their lips, and people respond to God in faith because of their relationship with such women. People, young and old, male and female will respond to Jesus because these women truly know Him. They are "Jesus with skin on" in the lives of others.

I believe since the Age of Enlightenment this relational aspect of the gospel has been pooh-poohed and shoved to the side. But the harvest has always had effective women laborers. Jesus' women pray for those around them and around the world. Sometimes we religious Christians focus on having all the intellectual ducks in a row, so to speak. We forget that simply being loved, noticed, and prayed for by someone who has found her life in Jesus is a powerful thing.

If you will notice as you read the Bible what it takes to be blessed of God, you will find it takes a lot less than you would think. Responding to God's love by faith and obedience is all that is required. Lots of busyness doing "churchy" things does not impress God. It never has. Trying to please other people with our show of religious zeal doesn't impress God either. We do not have to work so hard for God's favor. If we will simply believe what He says, He will restore us.

The restoration begins the moment a person reaches God through faith. It is safe to confess his/her need of forgiveness of sin. The process continues by the person's continued believing of God. God will finish the work He began in the heart. There is everlasting life for all who believe. Jesus will make all things new. A new heaven and new earth is coming. We will have freedom from the sin nature forever. Complete unity with God the Father, Son, and Holy Spirit as well as with each other is coming.

The one thing that counts is faith expressing itself through love. Faith opens the door of our hearts to His presence. Loving God and receiving His love through the indwelling Holy Spirit create the "rivers of living water" Jesus talked about. They flow from those who worship God in Spirit and in truth. It begins and continues in humble belief that we need saving and that God is the One who is rescuing us.

I have a picture in my mind of women in every country, every social strata, every economic condition lifting their hearts to their only Savior and living without apology for Him. Their chins are up and shoulders back. Their hands and loving words help many others. There is a light of hope in their eyes that does not come from this world. They are beautifully peaceful as they count on Him to be everything to them. They are happy to introduce another person to their Jesus. They do not cringe in the face of trouble. They stand in His grace, by His strength. They are noble women fulfilling their God-given role by simply walking with Him by faith.

May you, dear lady reader, and I always see Jesus. He is our life. He loves us deeply, daily, and without fail. Believe Him. We will meet in Heaven someday soon. Others who have believed on Him because of us will be there too. Because He has so loved us, we can love. May God richly bless us until we are safely at home together with Him.

Discussion Questions

1. Have you ever thought about the influence women have in people's lives? Satan wants it to be destructive. God, through Jesus, offers another kind of life to women everywhere. Which type of influence do you want to have on others? Evil or good, the choice is yours.

2. Have you ever thought of the relational nature of "missions"? How powerful is the influence of truth through a loving person? Will you let God love you so well that you will love others well?

Chapter Twenty

My Walk with Jesus

I was first introduced to Jesus by my wonderfully warm mother. I prayed at the age of three for Jesus to forgive my sin and come into my heart. I knew what it was to be bad, and what it meant to be spanked. I thought if Jesus wanted to take my spanking for me, I would certainly let Him.

At the age of seven a girlfriend of mine went to pray at the altar at the end of an evening church service. I went with her. God began to speak to me. "You can do anything you want to do with your life," He said, "But I have plans for you that I will help you follow if you choose to." I remember rocking back on my heels, since I was kneeling, shocked. I wondered if people actually made their own plans. How was I to know if I would be a good teacher, nurse, missionary, or store clerk? I had no idea! "Of course, I want Your plan, Lord. Whatever You want, I want what You want."

I grew up enjoying the friendships of my family and many, many people. Until I was 22 I had not really had any deep sorrows. Life was one sunny, wonderful place! I loved people, and they loved me. I loved life, and saw everything through eyes of possibility of what could be. I see God's mercy in all of that now. There were very deep waters ahead for me. There was much I had to go through to see more clearly the effects of evil in this world. So much hurt and pain. It was good that I had such a positive start for so long.

To live through what I term custom-designed crucibles caused my heart to cry out to my Jesus for rescue. At first I thought He would rescue me out of the trouble, but for the most part He has been my Rescuer through the trouble.

I have had three major themes of wrongness in my heart that I can see now at the age of 55. I lean on my own understanding of things. I care too much what other people think. And I lean on just about anything other than God for me to be OK, most of the time without knowing I am doing it.

I believe that God knows each of us intimately, that He truly did put us together in our mothers' wombs with the personalities, strengths and weaknesses we have. Our hearts are born with a strong independence from God. This is the essence of sin. We think we can do it on our own, and we surely do try, don't we? But since He made us and sees us perfectly, He can see what needs to be done in our lives to bring our hearts into healthy dependence and trust in Him. He is, I like to say, the perfect antidote for what is wrong in each of us. My life lessons may serve to encourage you, but your life's lessons will be custom tailored to your heart needs. Our lives are each unique stories of the rescue of God in real time in real human life. All of us are wrong. All of us need to connect to the Creator who made us, really deeply connect by faith alone or we will never know the life Jesus died for us to have. It is possible by faith to live a life of love, truth and light as we are going along.

So, in my life to correct my independence from Him, even though I sincerely wanted to please Him, God had to send paradigm-shifting trouble, confusion-creating enemies, and complete isolation. Every trial, trouble, suffering, hurt and pain has served to open my mind and heart to my huge need of Jesus to deliver me.

Nothing is by chance. God is not mad at me. He created me to walk with Him. Nothing else will ultimately satisfy me. That is so true. People, circumstances, and things can only satisfy me for a little while before my heart is empty again. But as I have pursued Him as my last resort and gotten glimpses of His magnificent heart, I have become addicted to Him. I cannot get enough of His love, wisdom, strength, power, understanding, truth, presence, patience, kindness, goodness, security, and comfort. He is everything I need in One Person. Father, Son and Holy Spirit not only understand the deepest longings of my heart, but the Lord meets those needs out of His own heart. He is what I crave. There is no one else like Him anywhere.

A word picture may help us to see what is going on in our lives. Because this world is so very dark, it is hard for us to know what in the world is going on. We are confused. We keep hitting brick walls and getting hurt. We do not understand life.

One scenario I love is that of a hostage rescue. You and I have been taken hostage by the enemy who hates us because God made us. We don't even know where we are, but we know we are in trouble. We are far away from anything that feels like home. The cruelty, lies, and manipulations of our captor make us feel like we are going crazy. We are fearful, defensively braced for anything, and becoming hopeless about ever getting free.

Then along comes the ultimate "special forces" guy. He knows where we are and where we came from. He knows the enemy very well. He has been dealing with him for a long time. He knows all his tricks. He knows not only the initial rescue procedure, but also the need for medical attention, food, rest, safety and care all the way back to our home. He has arranged for all of it. He has paid the expenses for the whole operation. He isn't just going to get us out of the bunker. He will take us from the holding cell, out of the building, out of the country, across the seas, and will not stop his protective care until we are all the way home. He is highly skilled, amazingly knowledgeable, incredibly strong, and tenderly understanding of what we have been through. He is a magnificent warrior. He is just who we need.

What is required of us? Once he breaks into our prison cell, he will identify himself, unchain us and ask us to follow him. Our part from that initial meeting through the long journey home is to trust him and do what he tells us to do. There may be times when he will tell us to "wait here," "stay down," "be quiet," or "don't move until I give the signal." We are never told to do anything we cannot do. Our trust in him is displayed by our obedience. That's it. That is all that is required of us. Everything else has been seen to. Our trust and obedience, our cooperation is imperative, however. Can you imagine what would happen if the hostage got all uppity and said, "I'll find my own way back, thank you very much."?

God never asked me to rescue myself. He doesn't expect me to know the darkness of my own heart. I am not responsible to be good enough to not need rescue. I do not know the way, the when, the how, or the what. The one thing I must stake my life on, and I do every day, is the Who. I believe with all my heart that Jesus is qualified to be my Rescuer. I believe He knows exactly what is going on at any given moment of time in my world. Nothing escapes His notice. He knows exactly what I am to do in response to the danger, too, and will tell me. I am getting better at asking, "What do You want me to do?"

He has promised never to leave me or forsake me. The rescue is not over . . . not until I am safely at Home in Heaven. Everything I will ever need to do what He asks me to do is already provided. It is given out on a daily basis. He is generous and sure in His leading of me. He knows all the pitfalls of my nature. He isn't going to lead me the way I think should go, but He will take me surely and safely to where I truly want to end up. I deeply long for the perfection of my Father's house. I want to be in a world where all is good, safe, happy, free, and beautiful. My heart longs to be a loving, secure place for others, to be one with the goodness of God. I do not like having to constantly fight my selfishness, pride, and ambitious expectations. My own heart is corrupt, but my Savior knows all about that. He is leading me out of my bondage and increasingly into the Light, my real home. My only job is to trust Him completely and do what He tells me to do by the strength He provides me. All is well. We are not there yet, but we are on the way. I am safe with Him, even if all around me is still foreign to my soul.

Sometimes I think of life as a story being written. I love to read stories where the main character has difficulties and challenges. I keep reading to see what will happen. How will he get out of this? But for my life I would rather live a boring happy little tale where nothing is ever hard. Is that not sad?

So, I am learning with every difficult disappointment or seemingly tragic turn of events to turn to my God and say, "Keep the pen in Your hand. Keep writing. I know this cannot be the end! I love reading Your other stories. I want to see how You are going to make my life a best-seller, too!"

One more picture. In the book of Daniel there is a story about three friends of Daniel who refuse to bow down and worship an image of the Babylonian king. They were ratted out and the king had the furnace heated seven times hotter than ever and had them thrown into it. This is where it is really interesting. The soldiers who threw them in were killed by the intense heat even at the furnace opening, but the three men were seen walking around inside the furnace with a fourth man who looked like "the son of God."

Eventually the king asked them to come back out of the furnace. The only things that burned were the ropes that bound them when they were thrown in. Not one hair was singed. Not one piece of their clothing was scorched. They didn't even smell like smoke. God had totally, completely delivered them . . . and kept them company inside the furnace. I want to be delivered like that!

I do not want the abuses, offenses, and enmity of others to cause me to be bitter, anxious, resentful or unforgiving. I want a clean, loving, joyful, peaceful, faith-filled heart that is enjoying His company no matter what else is going on . . . not even the smell of smoke. God can get me there. He can get us there. He is the same yesterday, today and forever. We can trust Him.

Author's Note

Thank you for reading. May God take you on your own adventure of rescue. May your heart find its safety in His. God bless you.